Valuation of Life Insurance Liabilities

Third Edition

Valuation of Life Insurance Liabilities

Third Edition

Mark A. Tullis, FSA, MAAA
Philip K. Polkinghorn, FSA, MAAA

ACTEX Publications
Winsted, Connecticut

Request for permission should be addressed to
        ACTEX Publications
        P.O. Box 974
        Winsted, CT 06098

Manufactured in the United States of America

10 9 8 7 6 5 4 3 2 1

Cover Design by MUF

Library of Congress Cataloging-in-Publication Data

Tullis, Mark A.
        Valuation of life insurance liabilities / Mark A. Tullis, Philip K.
Polkinghorn.
                p. cm.
                Includes bibliographical references.
                ISBN 1-56698-226-X
                1. Insurance, Life--Valuation--United States. 2. Insurance, Life--
Valuation--Canada. I. Polkinghorn, Philip K. II. Title.
HG8951.T85 1990
368.3'201--dc20   90-545
                                                                        CIP

ISBN: 1-56698-226-X

TABLE OF CONTENTS

PREFACE

The statutory valuation of life insurance liabilities has undergone a dramatic change since the mid-1970s. In Canada, rigid statutory requirements have been replaced with additional reliance on the judgment of the appointed actuary. In the U.S., the valuation actuary concept is a reality after years of discussion. In both the U.S. and Canada, new products have proliferated which are not easily valued using traditional valuation techniques. Fluctuating interest rates and increasing policy lapsation have placed greater emphasis on the proper matching of assets and liabilities.

This is a handbook of statutory valuation principles, with an emphasis on U.S. practices. Chapters 2 through 7 look at valuation requirements for traditional as well as "second generation" products and benefit riders. Chapters 8 and 9 examine the asset risk as it relates to liability valuation.

The authors thank John Brumbach, FSA, for providing valuable information and suggestions, as well as David Gershuni, FSA, FCIA, Michael Lombardi, FSA, FCIA, and Trevor Howes, FSA, FCIA, for the excellent material on Canadian valuation, much of which was used verbatim.

We also appreciate the editorial and design contributions made by the staff at ACTEX Publications, especially Marilyn J. Baleshiski, Denise Rosengrant, and Marlene Lundbeck who designed the cover for the text.

Atlanta and Lynchburg
July 1996

Mark A. Tullis, FSA, MAAA
Philip K. Polkinghorn, FSA, MAAA

To Helmut Koch and W. Robert Mann

CHAPTER ONE

TYPES OF VALUATIONS
AND BASIC REQUIREMENTS

A business cannot produce meaningful financial statements and balance sheets without accurate periodic assessments of its assets and liabilities. Valuing a typical business' liabilities generally presents few problems, as they consist primarily of accounts payable, indebtedness, unpaid taxes, and other items whose values can be readily determined using well established accounting principles. Furthermore, the size of these liabilities in relation to the earnings of the company is usually such that a small overstatement or understatement would not seriously distort earnings for a particular period. However, the principal liabilities of a life insurance company are due to the contingent benefits guaranteed in its long term policies and contracts. Over 85% of the liabilities of the typical life insurance company are life, health, or annuity reserves. Moreover, the magnitude of these reserves is such that a relatively small change in their value could significantly affect both earnings for a period and the equity value of the company. Consequently, the valuation and certification of these liabilities are among the more important actuarial functions for the typical life insurance company.

Reserves are liabilities for amounts an insurance company is obligated to pay in accordance with an insurance policy or annuity contract. The amounts are usually uncertain or contingent as to the exact amount and/or the time of payment (an exception being a reserve for an annuity-certain).

Some reserves are held because the event insured against has already happened, but the amount of claim is not known by the insurance company since the claim has not yet been reported to the company, or insufficient information has been furnished. Some reserves are held because the event insured against has not yet happened, but the insurance company is obligated to pay if the event does happen. The first kind of reserves are often called *claim reserves* or *loss reserves*, and the latter reserves are often called *policy reserves*.

This book is concerned with policy reserves for life insurance policies and annuities, including some miscellaneous benefits that are often included in such policies. The term *actuarial reserves* as used in this book means those policy reserves. Actuarial reserves are determined by performing an *actuarial valuation*.

A simple example is a single premium life insurance product, for which the company receives the entire premium at the issue date and must pay a death benefit at death sometime in the future. To recognize this obligation a reserve liability is established. As in this example, actuarial reserves involve the assessment of probabilities of future events, such as disability which may or may not arise; or the estimation of the timing of future events such as death, the eventual occurrence of which is a certainty. Actuarial reserves usually involve discounting to reflect the time value of money.[1]

Since reserves are calculated using probabilities of future events, they are subject to the Law of Large Numbers. In particular, reserves have true significance only for blocks of policies. Although as a practical matter, a reserve may be calculated for an individual policy, resulting in a real liability to the insurance company, the theory behind reserves only holds for large numbers of policies, and not at the individual policy level.

The valuation of the contingent liabilities of an insurance company involves placing a value on the present value of future events which sometimes cannot be predicted with much more than an educated guess. Results of an actuarial valuation can vary widely, not only because of the legitimately wide range of possible assumptions, but also because of variations in the methodology used to determine the value depending upon the purpose of the valuation. Because of this, it is important for the actuary to have a thorough awareness of the customary valuation methodologies available and their uses.

TYPES OF VALUATIONS

The methodology and assumptions appropriate for a valuation vary depending upon the purpose of the valuation.

---

[1] Although some types of "reserves," such as life claims incurred but not reported, may be calculated without discounting.

Statutory Valuations

Statutory valuations are performed to help insurance regulators assess the financial health of the life company. Because of the emphasis on determining solvency, U.S. statutory valuations tend to utilize conservative assumptions and techniques, thereby producing larger liabilities than if less conservative assumptions and techniques had been used.

In the U.S., the assumptions and methodology used to calculate minimum reserves in a statutory valuation are fairly explicit in the law. In other countries, such as Canada and the U.K., the actuary has more latitude in determining reserves. The required valuation methods in the U.S. are based largely on practical decisions that were made many years ago before the introduction of computers. For example, a statutory valuation is often thought of as a worst case scenario due to the conservative nature of the assumptions used and the fact that margins in future premiums are not always fully recognized. However, this is not an accurate picture, since, except for CARVM (the statutory annuity reserve method used in the U.S. described in Chapter 5), the level of future guaranteed nonforfeiture values is not explicitly taken into account in the determination of minimum statutory reserves.

Increasing reliance is being placed in the U.S. upon the valuation actuary. There is a trend away from viewing reserve liabilities as "cookbook" items, and toward the view that the actuary must seriously consider whether these liabilities make good and sufficient provision for all unmatured obligations of the company guaranteed under the terms of its policies. This trend is evident in the movement toward considering underlying assets in conjunction with the actuarial reserves of a company (such as has been the practice in the U.K. for decades, and, more recently, in Canada), and of the requirement of several states, most notably California, to require that actuarial reserves take due account of the nature of the underlying future guaranteed nonforfeiture values.

In Canada, much more responsibility is placed on the appointed actuary. Unlike the U.S., Canadian law does not require specific mortality tables or interest rates to be used in determining reserve liabilities. Rather, these assumptions are chosen by the actuary, subject to veto by the Superintendent of Insurance. Furthermore, as we shall see later, Canadian statutory valuations tend to more realistically reflect future liabilities under the contracts, with less emphasis placed on conservatism. Canadian actuaries must explicitly recognize the impact of lapses, and use of the prescribed reserving method (the Policy Premium Method or PPM) can produce negative terminal reserves.[2]

GAAP Valuations

For U.S. companies *GAAP valuations* are required if the company's stock is publicly traded in the U.S., or if the company is owned by a publicly traded company. GAAP accounting has as its objective the accurate allocation of income to the period in which it is earned. Thus, as opposed to U.S. statutory accounting, whose primary purpose is the assurance of solvency, there is less of an emphasis on conservative assumptions and methodology, although GAAP assumptions for traditional products are generally required to be "reasonable and conservative," and hence contain some element of conservatism. Like Canadian statutory accounting, GAAP valuation techniques incorporate explicit provision for lapses and surrender benefits, and frequently produce negative first year terminal reserves.[3]

In Canada, a single set of reserve values is used for both GAAP and statutory reporting. One of the primary motivations of adopting the Policy Premium Method, described in Chapter 2, was to eliminate differences between statutory and GAAP reserves.

Because U.S. statutory accounting may give a somewhat inaccurate view of the actual financial picture of a company, particularly with respect to trends,[4] many companies which are not required to produce GAAP financial statements (such as mutual companies) produce "GAAP-like" financials for the internal use of management to accurately assess the performance of the company. Typically these "GAAP-like" financials utilize GAAP principles modified to serve the needs of the individual company. An alternative approach for internal management reporting is the value-added financial measurement technique discussed briefly below, which is particularly attractive to mutual companies, since they are not restricted to the normal confines of GAAP accounting.

---

[2] However, there must be a surplus appropriation to offset any negative terminal reserves.

[3] Benefit reserves less unamortized deferred acquisition costs.

[4] For example, if a U.S. company were to stop writing new business in a given year, its statutory profits would typically increase over the prior year. Yet, sharp declines in new business production are generally not considered to be favorable occurrences.

Gross Premium Valuations

Gross premium valuations are generally performed when it is desirable to produce a "best estimate" value of the liabilities of the company, and hence may incorporate even less conservatism than GAAP valuations. Gross premium valuations may be appropriate when it is necessary to determine the value of a company, such as in the case of an acquisition or merger, or when a company is being examined in order to determine solvency. The Canadian Policy Premium Method (PPM) discussed in Chapter 2 is a gross premium valuation method.

As with GAAP, gross premium valuations incorporate explicit lapse assumptions. However, gross premium valuations are generally performed with "best estimate" assumptions, and little or no provision for conservatism. Unlike the valuation methods above, gross premium valuations offset the present value of future benefits and expenses payable with the present value of future *gross*, rather than net, premiums. The effect of this is that most or all future profits or losses are reflected in the equity of a gross premium valuation balance sheet as of the date of valuation.

An offshoot of the gross premium valuation is the ***value-added financial measurement*** technique, where financial performance of the company is measured by the change in value of the company, including change in total reserves and present value of future reserve increases. The value-added financial measurement approach utilizes year by year statutory reserve liabilities, but is like a gross premium valuation in that changes in the present value of future statutory profits are recognized as of the valuation date.

Tax Reserve Valuations

Tax reserve valuations are used in order to calculate the reserve liability for purposes of determining taxable income. In Canada, tax reserves are defined specifically in the tax code as one and one half year full preliminary term reserves with a cash surrender value floor.[5] Canadian tax reserves for a

---

[5] Under the tax basis assumptions, the present value at issue of policy premiums is required to cover the present value of benefits, outlays, and expenses. If the present value of the policy premiums is insufficient, the tax reserve interest rate must be increased until the test is satisfied.

specific policy may be either greater or less than statement reserves, depending upon the relationship of the assumptions.

In the U.S., tax reserves have historically been related to actual statutory reserves. From 1958 to 1984, tax reserves were based on the actual statutory reserves of the company, adjusted for some items, such as deficiency reserves,[6] which were specifically excluded for tax purposes. Because established companies frequently used more conservative reserving methods than new or growing companies, the prior law allowed restatement of tax reserves to a net level basis, using either exact or approximate methods. Another approximate formula was used to adjust the underlying reserve interest rate.

Congress perceived that this system was subject to abuse, compounded by the fact that the approximate recalculation methods specified in the law became less accurate as interest rates rose in the 1970's. Beginning in tax year 1984, the law was changed to require use of Federally Prescribed Tax Reserves (FPTR's) in the calculation of U.S. taxable income. Congress's intent was to completely specify the required methodology for calculation of tax reserves, so that two companies with identical policies in force would have identical tax reserves in any given tax year. Originally, FPTR's required the use of minimum permissible statutory reserves, using the highest interest rate and most recent mortality table allowed by at least 26 states. However, the law was later amended to require use of a prescribed tax interest rate, if greater. Some additional differences from statutory treatment are specified; for example, deficiency reserves are still not allowed.

The remainder of this text focuses on statutory treatment in the U.S. and Canada, with occasional comments as to differences in treatment of U.S. tax and statutory reserves.

EFFECTS OF STATUTORY RESERVE REQUIREMENTS

The level of statutory reserves has many effects on a company other than the obvious direct financial implications.

---

[6] Deficiency reserves were required (and still are in some cases) when the policy gross premium was less than the valuation net premium. They are discussed in detail in Chapter 7.

Gross Premium Levels

Although statutory reserve requirements do not directly affect the gross premiums charged by the company, they do indirectly. Generally, guaranteed premium levels are set so as to avoid deficiency reserves, and guaranteed fund accumulation rates for Universal Life policies are set at a level to avoid the analogous alternative minimum reserves. Also, when setting gross premium rates, companies must take into account the cost of capital required due to statutory reserve requirements.

Product Design

Aside from the design features inherent in the choice of guarantees as discussed above, statutory requirements often make otherwise desirable product features difficult or costly to reserve. Because of statutory reserve considerations, guaranteed cost of insurance rates for Universal Life policies are almost never less than rates based on the applicable valuation table. Aggressive term policies often feature guaranteed premium rates higher than those actually charged, primarily to avoid deficiency reserves. As a final example, interest guarantee structures of annuities can be influenced by CARVM reserve levels.

Federal Income Taxes

Under current Canadian law, life insurance tax reserves are defined independently from statutory reserves so the level of the latter will have little or no direct effect on income tax. However, Revenue Canada, the Canadian tax authority, is considering changing the tax reserve basis to 95% of statutory levels.[7]

In the U.S., Federal Income Taxes are fairly insensitive to the actual statutory reserve level, as Federally Prescribed Tax

Reserves are defined separately in the tax code. However, the choice of a statutory reserve basis still has several minor effects on tax reserves. Items unspecified in the tax code, such as whether tax reserves are calculated on a continuous or curtate basis, should follow the statutory practice for the plan in question. Also, in the U.S., tax reserves for a policy may not exceed statutory reserves. Thus, the choice of a statutory basis which results in lower reserves

---

[7] Also note that, for tax purposes, the allocation of investment income of multinational Canadian companies, and hence their taxable profits in Canada, is currently based on statutory reserves.

than would be required on the Federally Prescribed basis would result in lower tax reserves than if a more conservative basis were used.

Dividends to Policyholders

There are many techniques used by companies to calculate policyholder dividends, but many companies use two or three factor formula methods utilizing the statutory reserve as an input item in the calculation of the interest and mortality components. Where this is the case, the choice of statutory reserve basis will have a significant effect on how dividends are distributed on a durational basis and among the various classes of policyholders. Even if a company uses another method to calculate dividends, choice of a statutory reserve basis will enter into the calculation and allocation of surplus, thereby indirectly affecting distribution of dividends.

Statutory Earnings

The fact that statutory reserves affect statutory earnings is obvious in itself, but it leads to several interesting corollaries. In the U.S., the amount of money which may be paid out as dividends to stockholders is generally limited by the accumulated statutory earnings of the company.[8] This makes the realistic projection of statutory earnings the basis of determining the appraisal value of a life company since the economic value of the company is most directly related to the present value of distributable earnings. It also means that the incidence of statutory earnings, and hence the appraisal value of the company, will be affected by the statutory reserve basis.

Important Indicators

Several important indicators used within the industry to measure the strength of companies[9] are based in part upon statutory financial measures, and many companies manage their business, including the selection of the statutory reserve basis, so that these indicators are as favorable as possible.

---

[8] In Canada, the dividends payable to stockholders from earnings on participating policies is limited to 2.5% to 10% of statutory par earnings, depending on the size of the mean par fund. Essentially no limitations are placed on dividends payable from non-par earnings in Canada.

[9] For example, the indicators used by many of the rating agencies.

Other Considerations

There is at least one other way that the choice of statutory reserve basis can affect the apparent, if not actual, profitability of a life policy. Many companies, particularly mutuals, use a profit objective which requires that accumulated surplus divided by statutory reserves must be at least equal to a specified level (say 5%) at the end of a given duration such as the 20th. For such a company, the level of the statutory reserve in the target year will have a direct effect on the plan's perceived profitability.

It is important to remember that the reserving method and basis do not directly affect the total profitability of a policy, only the emergence of profit by year. It can be shown that if two alternative sets of reserves for a policy grade together at the maturity date, the pre-tax profits produced by the two will have the same present value at issue, assuming the interest rate used to discount is the same rate at which investment income is calculated. However, if a higher interest rate is used to discount, the set of reserves which are generally lower will produce the largest present value of profits.

VALUATION REQUIREMENTS

There are at least three major components of any statutory valuation.

Mathematical Calculations

The first component of a statutory valuation is the mathematical calculation of the present value of the excess of future benefits over future premiums under the contracts. This exercise is based on assumptions as to lapses (which may be zero, as under U.S. statutory valuation), mortality, interest, etc., and is covered in Chapters 2 and 3 for traditional products, Chapter 4 for interest sensitive life products, Chapter 5 for annuities, and Chapter 6 for variable products.

Verification of Results

Additional emphasis in statutory valuation has recently been placed on the demonstration that assumptions are reasonable for the particular valuation. In particular, there has been recent concern as to whether the interest assumption is appropriate. The view has emerged that it is not sufficient to examine the assets separately in order to determine the appropriate interest assumption for the valuation; rather, the structure of the assets must be viewed together with the structure of the liabilities in order to determine the interest assumptions appropriate for the valuation. This problem is discussed in greater detail in Chapters 8 and 9.

Actuarial Opinion

In both the United States and Canada, a qualified actuary signs an actuarial opinion as to the appropriateness of the reserves. This is discussed in detail in the remainder of this chapter.

VALUATION REQUIREMENTS IN THE UNITED STATES

In 1990 the NAIC adopted a revised model Standard Valuation Law which requires an Actuarial Opinion of Reserves to be filed annually. According to the 1990 SVL,

> "Every life insurance company doing business in this state shall annually submit the opinion of a qualified actuary as to whether the reserves and related actuarial items held in support of the policies and contracts ... are computed appropriately, are based on assumptions which satisfy contractual provisions, are consistent with prior reported amounts, and comply with applicable laws of this state. The commissioner by regulation shall define the specifics of this opinion and add any other items deemed to be necessary to its scope."

The statement of actuarial opinion should list the items and amounts for which the actuary expresses an opinion. There may be separate opinions for separate blocks of business; for example one actuary may sign an opinion relating to group insurance items, while another signs an opinion relating to individual life insurance, and a third actuary signs an opinion relating to individual health insurance items. Note, however that the opinion is on the adequacy of reserves in aggregate, and that it is possible for deficiencies in individual components of the reserves to be offset by margins in other items.

The statement of actuarial opinion frequently indicates reliance on others. For example, it may indicate reliance on others within the company for the accuracy and completeness of the basic records, and reliance on actuaries with other companies for items such as reinsurance assumed. The statement of actuarial opinion should indicate the relationship of the actuary with the company, and the scope of the actuary's work.

The American Academy of Actuary's Recommendation 7, and Interpretations 7-A, 7-B, and 7-C deal with the statement of actuarial opinion in greater depth and define in greater detail what is required on the actuary's part. Interpretation 7-A discusses the situation where the statement of actuarial opinion indicates reliance on others. Interpretation 7-C discusses the situation where the actuary's opinion must be qualified.

Prior to adoption of the 1990 SVL, it was generally held that in the case of ambiguities, the requirements of the company's state of domicile determined the appropriate reserve level. The new Actuarial Opinion of Reserves differs from prior practice in that the statement reserves as filed in any particular state, in the aggregate, must satisfy the laws of that state, and presumably also satisfy the regulations of that particular insurance department. Because numerous ambiguities in the standard valuation law are interpreted many different ways by the various departments, this leads to a practical problem in determining reserve levels under the new law, and raises the possibility that a company would, in theory, effectively be required either to calculate reserves for various blocks of policies several ways, incorporating all of the different interpretations and taking the largest aggregate total, or else to use the most conservative interpretation for each individual item in question.

The 1990 SVL also requires an actuarial analysis of reserves and assets supporting such reserves. This requirement is discussed in Chapter 9.

Opinion as to Nonguaranteed Elements

In addition to the basic U.S. reserve opinion, the actuary must answer the following question on Page 11 after Exhibit 8A of the standard NAIC convention blank:

"Does the company at present issue or have in force policies that contain nonguaranteed elements?"

Such contracts include, but are not limited to, the following if they contain nonguaranteed elements:

(1) Single and periodic premium deferred annuities.
(2) Universal Life contracts providing for fixed and/or flexible premiums.
(3) Adjustable periodic premium life contracts, also known as indeterminate premium life contracts.
(4) Single and periodic premium life contracts.
(5) Renewable and convertible term insurance contracts which do not guarantee the premiums payable upon renewal, or which provide for renewal on the then current premium basis.

According to the Actuarial Standards Board (ASB) recommendations concerning contracts with nonguaranteed elements, nonguaranteed elements are "charges or benefits [which] may vary at the discretion of the company... they do not apply to policyholder dividends." According to the annual statement instructions, "the term 'nonguaranteed' does not apply to charges or benefits that contractually follow a separate account result or a defined index."

An affirmative answer to this question requires the following items to be included with the annual statement:

(1) A statement containing the determination procedures for the nonguaranteed elements.
(2) Eight interrogatories dealing with determination of the nonguaranteed elements, supportability of the current level of nonguaranteed elements, and relationship of the nonguaranteed elements currently charged or supportable to those used in sales illustrations.
(3) An actuarial opinion relating to nonguaranteed elements to be signed by a member of the American Academy of Actuaries.

The actuary signing the nonguaranteed element opinion must be familiar with the company's pricing and repricing assumptions illustration practices, and actual experience relative to lapse, mortality, interest earnings, and expenses.

Risk Based Capital Requirements

To function as an ongoing concern and to allow for the various risks associated with the business of insurance, life insurance companies need surplus in addition to their required statutory reserves.

Beginning in 1994, the NAIC has required calculation of *Risk Based Capital* (RBC) using a prescribed method. RBC is a representation of a "minimum" capital and surplus level for a particular company, taking into account the particular risks to which the company is exposed. RBC has components representing a company's

(1) asset quality and payment default risk,
(2) insurance risk,
(3) interest rate risk, and
(4) business risk.

The formula used is nonlinear to allow for risk correlations among the various components.

The *RBC ratio* is a company's actual adjusted capital and surplus divided by the company's RBC. The RBC ratios are used by the NAIC to evaluate the surplus adequacy of life insurance companies. If a company's RBC ratio falls below a specified level, certain "action levels" are triggered, ranging from a "mandatory control level" where the insurance commissioner must seize control of the company, to a "trend test level" where the company must perform an additional test to determine recent trends in the RBC ratios.

VALUATION REQUIREMENTS IN CANADA

In June 1979, the Canadian Institute of Actuaries (the Institute) issued "Recommendations for Insurance Company Financial Reporting" governing the conduct of a member acting in the capacity of a valuation actuary for an insurance company. The Institute's objectives were to ensure that actuarial information be properly determined and fully disclosed, and that both information and disclosure be capable of judgment by peers as good actuarial practice and merit the respect and acceptance by the public and Superintendents of Insurance. The Recommendations are accompanied by nonbinding Explanatory Notes intended to amplify the Recommendations or to illustrate their application. The Recommendations deal with the verification of valuation data, the development of appropriate assumptions, the choice of valuation method, and the text and implications of the reports accompanying the published financial statements and government statement. They also touch on documentation of the valuation actuary's work, the use of approximations, and judgment regarding materiality.

While the recommendations provide sound general guidance for the practicing valuation actuary, they are most easily and directly interpreted in the context of traditional ordinary life insurance.

However, there is a wide range of types of policies included in a typical valuation today. They present a variety of technical problems that are difficult to resolve by a straightforward interpretation of professional standards. To assist the valuation actuary with such technical problems, the Canadian Institute of Actuaries (CIA) has issued a series of Valuation Technique Papers (VTP's). Once adopted these papers are binding on actuaries performing policy valuations for Canadian financial statements.

Valuation Technique Papers have been issued on the following topics to date:

(1)   Valuation of Lapse Supported Products
(2)   Valuation of Individual Renewal Term Insurance
(3)   Future Cash Flow Investment Assumption for Ordinary Life Insurance Valuation
(4)   Valuation of Reinsured Policies
(5)   Valuation of Adjustable Products
(6)   Expected Mortality Experience for Individual Insurance
(7)   Group Life and Health
(8)   Reserving for AIDS
(9)   Valuation of Single Premium Annuities
(10) Valuation of Participating Policies
(11) Valuation of Universal Life Policies
(12) Valuation of Individual A&S Insurance Issued by Life Insurers
(13) A&S Expected Experience
(14) Valuation of Insured Claims Liabilities
—   VTP on Wind-up & Solvency Valuation (unnumbered)

Eight of the first nine papers were binding as of December 1995, the exception being the paper on group life and health,

In addition to Technique Papers, the CIA has released "Guidance Notes for the Valuation Actuary" to assist in dealing with financial reporting issues related to AIDS. The Guidance Notes, which supplement Valuation Technique Paper No. 8, are descriptions of acceptable practice in dealing with a difficult issue. Furthermore, actuaries were expected to comply with the recommendations contained in these Guidance Notes, as indicated in the annual memorandum to valuation actuaries issued by the federal Office of the Superintendent of Financial Institutions.

The CIA has also issued a Provisions for Adverse Deviations Paper which is designed to go hand in hand with the VTPs. PPM reserves are required to use assumptions allowing for *provisions for adverse deviations* (PAD's). If the PAD's are set too high, reserves are too high and profits are deferred; if PAD's are too low, reserves are too low and profits are released too quickly. This paper was released to provide guidance to the actuary in setting acceptable PAD's for each of the critical actuarial valuation assumptions: 1) mortality, 2) lapses, 3) expenses, and 4) interest rates. This paper provides for a range of high and low PAD's acceptable for each assumption, with the actuary responsible for selecting the specific PAD appropriate for the circumstances at hand.

In addition to providing formal standards of practice and guidance material as described above, the CIA has taken steps to monitor compliance with its standards of practice by members acting as valuation actuaries. All valuation actuaries must complete and sign a two-part questionnaire which covers a variety of issues related to compliance with actuarial standards of practice for the statutory valuation process just completed. Only one of the two parts is required to be submitted to the Institute, and the other may remain on file at the company.

Recent Developments in Canada

There are a number of significant recent developments affecting Canadian actuaries, including the following:

(1) A new Insurance Companies Act
(2) Standards of Practice for the Appointed Actuary
(3) The Policy Premium Method (PPM) of Valuation
(4) Minimum Continuing Capital and Surplus Requirements (MCCSR)
(5) Dynamic Solvency Testing (DST)
(6) Joint Policy Statement

Insurance Companies Act

A new Insurance Companies Act came into force in 1992 redefining the regulation of insurance companies and more specifically creating the role of appointed actuaries. The appointed actuary has been given broad roles and responsibilities similar in concept to those of the appointed actuary in the United Kingdom:

(1) Appointments will be made and terminated by the board of directors, and the actuary will have access to the board.

(2) The actuary will value and report on actuarial and other policy benefit liabilities.

(3) The actuary will report annually to the board of directors on the current financial position of the company.

(4) The actuary may be directed by regulation to report on the future financial condition of the company.

(5) The actuary is to have access to all necessary company records and information required in the performance of assigned duties.

(6) If the actuary becomes aware of any circumstances that may have a material impact on the ability of the company to meet its obligations and which require rectification, he or she must bring the matter to the attention of management and the board.

(7) If satisfactory action is not taken to correct the situation within a reasonable period of time, the actuary will have a statutory obligation to send a copy of his or her report to the Superintendent of Financial Institutions and so advise the board of directors.

(8) The actuary is to render an opinion to the board on the administration of the company dividend policy prior to any distributions.

Standards of Practice for the Appointed Actuary

In conjunction with the new role of appointed actuary, the CIA has issued "Standards of Practice for the appointed actuary of an Insurance Company" which govern the conduct of the actuary in such matters as appointment, access to information, management reporting, board reporting and financial statements. A separate standard of practice was issued governing "The Appointed Actuary's Report for Insurance Company Financial Statements" and covers primarily the report language to be used in published financial statements.

The Policy Premium Method

A key element of the new GAAP and statutory principles is the requirement to use the *Policy Premium Method* of valuation (PPM) for both GAAP and statutory reporting. The PPM is a prospective method of valuation which uses

(1) the full gross premium for the policy, and
(2) the estimated expenses and obligations under the policy (without arbitrary limitations).

More details on this method and on setting assumptions for use under PPM are covered in Chapter 2.

Companies registered in Quebec have been operating under the PPM environment since 1991, and federally registered companies are expected to do so in 1992, once the PPM is endorsed by the federal Superintendent of Financial Institutions.

Minimum Continuing Capital and Surplus Requirements

The calculation of actuarial liabilities serve a dual purpose: to provide for future obligations on the balance sheet, and to appropriately charge income in the income statement. Canadian statutory valuations had in the past been performed primarily to meet the concerns of regulators that companies remain solvent. This is why, until recently, prescribed Canadian valuation methods and assumptions have been conservative.

The movement in Canada to make actuarial liabilities appropriate for both statutory and GAAP purposes has necessitated a fresh look at how management and regulators can be assured that a company will remain solvent.

The Canadian Life and Health Insurance Association (CLHIA) has implemented a policyholder protection plan administered by a specially established corporation known as COMPCORP. Companies who write direct business are required by all provincial jurisdictions to join this plan. They must pass, on an annual basis, a formula-based test known as the *Minimum Continuing Capital and Surplus Requirement* (MCCSR). The MCCSR is similar to the NAIC's Risk Based Capital requirements for US companies, in that it compares actual adjusted capital and surplus to minimum requirements. Like the NAIC RBC, MCCSR takes into account each company's approximate risk factors based upon that company's asset and liability portfolios.

The form developing the company's MCCSR ratio must be signed by the Appointed Actuary as well as an official designated by the company's board of directors. The form must be submitted to the federal Office of Financial Institutions (OSFI) together with the company's Annual Statement.

Dynamic Solvency Testing

The Canadian Institute of Actuaries created a Committee on Solvency Standards to study the actuarial aspects of corporate solvency and to provide guidance to actuaries practicing in this area. Accordingly, a standard of practice was adopted, effective with the 1991 year-end, which requires the actuary to examine not only the company's current financial position, but also its financial condition, including its ability to withstand future threats to solvency.

The actuary's annual investigation of the company's solvency should consider the past, present and future financial positions of the company and the sensitivity of surplus to changes in various experience factors and management policies. In addition to the base scenario normally underlying the company's business plan, a minimum of 10 other scenarios are suggested for investigation (worse than expected mortality, morbidity, withdrawals, expenses, changing investment yields, and so on), as well as any additional or integrated scenarios which the actuary considers appropriate to the circumstances. Investigations should include both the business in force and anticipated new business. Finally, the actuary should provide a written report to the board of directors each year outlining the investigation performed and presenting the significant findings and conclusions.

Joint Policy Statement

An insurance company's auditor relies on the actuary for many items in the balance sheet and year-to-year changes in these liabilities implicit in the income statement. The actuary may in turn rely upon the auditor's verification of data on which the policy valuation is based.

A Joint Policy Statement was issued by the Canadian Institute of Actuaries and the Canadian Institute of Chartered Accountants in 1991 to address how the actuary and auditor should interact in meeting their professional responsibilities and how their roles should be disclosed to readers of financial statements.

The Joint Policy Statement recognizes that either the actuary or the auditor could be using the specialized work of the other, and outlines the following four aspects of the work that should be considered when preparing a report relying on such work:

(1) The specialist professional's qualifications, competence, integrity, and objectivity.
(2) The specialist professional's appointment to do the work.
(3) Whether the specialist professional has followed the standards of his or her profession in carrying out the work.
(4) The appropriateness of the specialist professional's findings and opinions.

In addition to the report of the auditor and the report of the actuary, the new legislation requires a statement of management describing the respective roles of the auditor and the actuary.

***

Overall, in recent years statutory valuation has received increased attention worldwide. In the United Kingdom, significant reliance has long been placed on the actuary's professional judgement. In Canada, developments over the years have created a very similar role for the appointed actuary. The recent emphasis in the United States on the role of the valuation actuary serves to underline the importance of statutory valuation to the life insurance industry in that country.

EXERCISES

1. In the U.S., statutory reserves are deliberately set at conservative levels due to solvency concerns. In Canada, statutory reserves are more like U.S. GAAP reserves, which are on a more "realistic" basis.

   (a) Discuss recent action taken in Canada to help ensure solvency, within the less conservative reserve environment.
   (b) Discuss recent U.S. action taken with a view toward ensuring the solvency of life companies.

2. A company is considering a change in its reserve basis for new policies, resulting in lower reserves. Discuss the implications of this change.

3. Compare the requirements of the valuation actuary in the U.S. to those of the appointed actuary in Canada.

CHAPTER TWO

RESERVE METHODOLOGIES AND BASES

VALUATION STANDARDS IN THE UNITED STATES

In the U.S., acceptable reserve methodologies and bases are determined as of the policy issue date by the state valuation laws then in effect. While specific valuation requirements can vary from state to state, all states have adopted some form of the Standard Valuation Law (SVL), which was developed by the National Association of Insurance Commissioners (NAIC) to provide uniformity.

The SVL is amended from time to time. The most recent amendments have been the 1976 Amendments, the 1980 Amendments, and the 1990 Amendments to the SVL. The SVL has consistently defined minimum reserves in terms of a net premium valuation.

The SVL also sets forth the minimum standards of mortality and interest that may be used in calculating statutory reserves. To give an idea how the bases have changed over the years, Appendix A shows the prevailing state interest rates and mortality tables in effect over the past 30 years.

Since the 1980 Amendments, the SVL has used dynamic valuation interest rates that are meant to adjust valuation bases for changes in interest rates more quickly than was previously possible.

Prior to the 1980 Amendments, a change in the maximum valuation interest rate would have required each state to pass an amendment to the SVL.

VALUATION BASES IN THE UNITED STATES

Valuation Mortality

Prior to the 1980 Amendments to the SVL, minimum standards of valuation mortality for life policies were stated in terms of attained age mortality tables with age setbacks used to reflect differences in mortality between males and females. With the adoption of the 1980 CSO table as specified in the 1980 Amendments, the situation is more complicated. For example, in a number of states, the valuation actuary has a choice of the following tables for life products:

(1) The regular 1980 CSO Mortality Table, both male and female versions.
(2) Smoker and nonsmoker versions of the 1980 CSO Mortality Table for each sex.
(3) Unisex versions of the 1980 CSO Mortality Table.[1]
(4) Unisex smoker and nonsmoker versions of the 1980 CSO Mortality Table.

Of course, all of the above tables are available in both age last and age nearest birthday versions. Additionally, all may be modified by use of optional 10-year or 15-year select factors.

It should be noted that the 1980 Amendments to the SVL prescribe different minimum standards of mortality for males and females, except when unisex tables are allowed. Although, unisex tables are allowed in all states for nonforfeiture purposes, several states require reserves for unisex products to be calculated using separate mortality for males and females.

Prior to the 1980 Amendments, the SVL allowed only a three year age setback for female issues prior to 1977, and a six year age setback for female issues thereafter. In developing the 1980 CSO Mortality Table, it was noted that the actual theoretical age setback varied by age and that use of a single age setback could be inappropriate in certain circumstances. Also, more and more insurance was being sold to female lives, providing both a greater need for a separate table and more experience upon which such a table could be based. These facts led to the development of a separate version of the 1980 CSO Mortality Table for females.

---

[1] Various unisex versions are available, depending on the expected mix by sex.

Interest Rates

Between 1947 and 1974, most states used a 3.5% valuation interest rate in defining the minimum valuation standard for all classes of insurance and annuities.

Historically, the average net investment rate of life insurance companies reached historic lows in the 1940's. During this period, many companies strengthened reserves on old blocks of business by decreasing the valuation interest rates, and valuation interest rates for new business of 2% to 3% were not uncommon. Later, as new money rates improved and life insurance portfolio earnings increased, companies began to use higher valuation interest rates but were constrained by the legal maximum of 3.5%.

Eventually, companies were forced to reflect the higher available investment earnings in their premium rates even though they were unable to reflect these higher earnings in their reserve calculations. As a result, annual premium products often required deficiency reserves, and single premium products were sold at premium rates lower than the reserves required at issue. In response, the NAIC adopted more liberal valuation bases in line with the higher interest earnings. It is important to note that the changes made at this time began to reflect the differing investment risks associated with different product lines, as well as the increasing importance of annuities in the marketplace. For example, the maximum statutory valuation rate for group annuities and single premium immediate annuities was increased to 6% but the maximum statutory valuation interest rate for life insurance and deferred annuities was increased only to 4%. Previously, the maximum valuation interest rate was identical for all lines of business.

In December of 1976, the NAIC further changed the model SVL and even higher valuation interest rates were adopted with the rate for life insurance raised to 4.5%. Also, a provision in the SVL that would otherwise have required statutory valuation interest rates to revert to 3.5% on January 1, 1986 was removed.

The 1980 Amendments to the SVL contain dynamic maximum valuation interest rates which are a function of the Monthly Average of the Composite Yield on Seasoned Corporate Bonds, as published by Moody's Investors Service, Inc. Resulting rates for life policies vary by guarantee duration, where, for life insurance, guarantee duration is the maximum number of years the life insurance can remain in force on a basis guaranteed in the policy or under options to convert to plans of life insurance with premium rates or nonforfeiture values or both which are guaranteed in the original policy. Separate rates result for guarantee durations of 10 or less, 11 through 20, and more than 20, with rates lower for longer guarantee durations. Chapter 5 discusses maximum valuation interest rates for annuities allowed by the 1980 Amendments. An historical presentation of prevailing minimum valuation interest rates is shown in Appendix A.

RESERVE METHODS IN THE UNITED STATES

Net Level Premium Reserve Method

The *net level premium reserve method* uses net premiums designed to cover benefits only. No explicit recognition of any expenses is made. For a given plan and issue age, net premiums are set equal to a constant percentage of gross premiums according to the formula

$$\sum_{t=1} K \cdot GP_t \cdot v^{t-1} \cdot \frac{\ell_{x+t-1}}{\ell_x} = \sum_{t=1} DB_t \cdot v^t \cdot \frac{d_{x+t-1}}{\ell_x}, \qquad (2.1)$$

where
$$NP_t = K \cdot GP_t. \qquad (2.2)$$

For a whole life contract we have

$$NP = P_x = \frac{A_x}{\ddot{a}_x}. \qquad (2.3)$$

The net level premium reserve method typically produces the highest reserves of any of the methods discussed in this book. Unlike most other reserving methods, the net level method typically requires a significant first year reserve and is therefore avoided by surplus-conscious companies.

Expense Allowances

Some reserve methods contain an *expense allowance* or *expense adjustment*. An expense allowance is used to reflect the fact that most life insurance sales involve large first year expenses which are intended to be recovered from future margins. The expense allowance is an offset to the reserve and is amortized over some period.

Modified reserves can generally be thought of as net level reserves less an unamortized expense allowance.[2] If we define the expense allowance as

$$EA = \beta_x^{MOD} - \alpha_x^{MOD}, \tag{2.4}$$

where β_x^{MOD} is the renewal net premium for the modified reserve method and α_x^{MOD} is the first year net premium, then

$$V^{MOD} = V^{NL} - EA\left(\frac{\ddot{a}_{x+t}}{\ddot{a}_x}\right), \tag{2.5}$$

where $\ddot{a}_x$ is a generalized expression for an annuity reflecting the pattern (level or otherwise) and duration of premium payments. Frequently, particularly in Canada, the expense allowance has been thought of in other terms.[3] However, in the discussion of U.S. methods which follows, the expense allowance is assumed to be the difference between the renewal and first year modified net premiums.

Full preliminary term (FPT) *reserves* use a first year net premium equal to the one-year-term net premium and a renewal net premium equal to the net level premium for the remaining coverage at the original issue age plus 1. Thus, for a whole life contract,

$$EA = \frac{A_{x+1}}{\ddot{a}_{x+1}} - c_x, \tag{2.6}$$

where $c_x = A^1_{x:\overline{1}|}$. This results in a first year terminal reserve of zero.

For statutory valuations there is a limit on the maximum expense allowance. This limit helps to define minimum reserves as explained below. Note, however, that the expense allowance is formula-based, and is not limited by the actual first-year expenses incurred.

---

[2] The deferred acquisition cost asset established as a part of U.S. GAAP is essentially equivalent to an expense allowance.

[3] For example, if the expense allowance is denoted EA' and if it is defined as $EA' = P_x^{NL} - \alpha_x^{MOD}$, then $V^{MOD} = V^{NL} - EA'\left(\frac{\ddot{a}_{x+t}}{\ddot{a}_x}\right)$.

Commissioners Reserve Valuation Method (CRVM)

The reserve method producing the smallest reserves allowed by the SVL is the *Commissioners Reserve Valuation Method* (CRVM). The CRVM requires FPT reserves for plans if the resulting FPT adjusted net premiums are not greater than 20-pay-life adjusted FPT net premiums. For plans with adjusted net premiums larger than the 20-pay-life adjusted net premium, the expense deferral is limited to $_{19}P_{x+1} - c_x$.

In the case of a policy with non-level death benefits, Actuarial Guideline XVII[4] suggests $_{19}P_{x+1}$ be calculated assuming a level death benefit equal to the arithmetic average of the death benefit at the beginning of policy years 2 through 10, inclusive. Valuation net premiums in years two and later are a constant percentage of gross premiums. This percentage, K, is found from the formula

$$\sum_{t=1} K \cdot GP_t \cdot v^{t-1} \cdot \frac{\ell_{x+t-1}}{\ell_x}$$
$$= \left[\sum_{t=1} DB_t \cdot v^t \cdot \frac{d_{x+t-1}}{\ell_x}\right] + {_{19}P_{x+1}} - DB_1 \cdot c_x, \quad (2.7a)$$

if $P^{FPT} > {_{19}P_{x+1}}$, or from

$$\sum_{t=2} K \cdot GP_t \cdot v^{t-1} \cdot \frac{\ell_{x+t-1}}{\ell_x} = \sum_{t=2} DB_t \cdot v^t \cdot \frac{d_{x+t-1}}{\ell_x} \quad (2.7b)$$

if $P^{PFT} < {_{19}P_{x+1}}$.

Formulas (2.7a) and (2.7b) are generalized to allow for varying death benefit or premium patterns.[5]

Actuarial Guideline XXV defines, for reserve calculations, an assumed future death benefit increase for policies whose premiums are fixed at issue

---

[4] Actuarial Guidelines are developed by the NAIC to "promote uniformity in regulation which is beneficial to everyone." In most states actuarial guidelines are not law or regulation and they "are not intended to be viewed as statutory revisions, but merely a guide to be used in applying a statute to a specific circumstance." (Quotes from *Financial Condition Examiners Handbook*.)

[5] However, Actuarial Guideline XXI states that if the resulting $\beta - \alpha$ is negative, then the excess is to be taken as zero. Actuarial Guideline XXI also states that a literal interpretation of the Standard Valuation Law requires an adjustment to Formula (2.7b) if $GP_1 \neq GP_2$.

and which provide for whole life insurance with the amount of death benefit adjusted periodically with the Consumer Price Index or some other cost-of-living index. This assumed future increase is equal to the valuation rate for the policy minus a constant based on the type of guarantee in the contract.

As the above formulas indicate, the net premiums are dependent on the slope of the gross premium scale. However, except in situations where deficiency reserves are required, the magnitude of the gross premiums does not affect the level of net premiums or reserves.

The CRVM produces a first-year terminal reserve of zero for a large number of policies, thus reducing the statutory surplus strain associated with the sale of new business.

Other Methods

Other modified reserve methods are in use. One of the more common alternatives is a method in which reserves grade from CRVM to net level at some duration. A major reason for such a method is that many companies want to offer products with 20th year cash values that are higher than minimum cash values yet not greater than the reserve held.

An example of the calculations of net premiums and reserves for a whole life plan with reserves that are CRVM at the end of year one, grading to net level reserves at year twenty, is given below.

Issue Age 35
Reserve Basis: 1958 CSO
Age Last Birthday
Valuation Interest: 4.0%

$$\text{CRVM Net Premium} = P^{CRVM} = 1000 \cdot \frac{A_{x+1}}{\ddot{a}_{x+1}} = 14.867$$

$${}_1V_x^{MOD} = 0 = A_{x+1} - \frac{A_{x+1}}{\ddot{a}_{x+1}} \cdot \ddot{a}_{x+1}$$

$$= A_{x+1} - P^G \cdot \ddot{a}_{x+1:\overline{19|}} - P^{NL} \cdot {}_{19|}\ddot{a}_{x+1}$$

$$\text{Graded Net Premium} = P^G$$

$$= 1000 \cdot \frac{A_{x+1} - \left(\frac{A_x}{\ddot{a}_x}\right){}_{19|}\ddot{a}_{x+1}}{\ddot{a}_{x+1:\overline{19|}}} = 15.142$$

$$_tV_{35} = 1000 \cdot A_{x+t} - \left[\sum_{s=t}^{19} P^G \cdot v^{s-t} \cdot \frac{\ell_{x+s}}{\ell_{x+t}} + \sum_{s=20}^{\omega-x-1} P^{NL} \cdot v^{s-t} \cdot \frac{\ell_{x+s}}{\ell_{x+t}} \right]$$

$$_1V_{35}^{CRVM} = 0.00 \qquad _{10}V_{35}^{CRVM} = 127.28 \qquad _{20}V_{35}^{CRVM} = 296.25$$

$$_1V_{35}^{NL} = 12.24 \qquad _{10}V_{35}^{NL} = 137.96 \qquad _{20}V_{35}^{NL} = 304.85$$

$$_1V_{35}^{G} = 0.00 \qquad _{10}V_{35}^{G} = 130.36 \qquad _{20}V_{35}^{G} = 304.85$$

A simpler way to solve for the grading net premium would be to use the relationship between the net premium and the expense allowance. We know that the present value of the difference between valuation net premiums and net level premiums equals the expense allowance remaining, so that

$$(P^G - P^{NL}) \cdot \ddot{a}_{x+1:\overline{19|}} = EA^{CRVM} \left(\frac{\ddot{a}_{x+1}}{\ddot{a}_x} \right). \tag{2.8}$$

In general, a net premium reserve method is defined by the magnitude of the expense allowance and the period over which the expense allowance is amortized. Although the above example began to grade to net level in the second policy year, it is possible for the reserve to equal CRVM for a number of years before the grading begins.

Other Alternatives

Some actuaries believe that major revisions to the standard valuation law are necessary. Among their arguments are the following:

(1) The SVL is based on artificial, predetermined interest rates fixed over the life of the contract.
(2) The conservatism embedded in the SVL was deliberately intended to introduce an implicit solvency margin related to the volume of business transacted. This conservatism is in addition to the explicit Risk Based Capital required, as discussed in Chapter 1.
(3) As a practical matter, we now know that the SVL does not fully achieve this purpose; several recent insolvencies illustrate the point.

Those who feel the current SVL does not work well vary in their proposed remedies. One reaction has been to require the actuary to perform dynamic valuations to measure the ability of reserves to meet the asset risk. These valuations supplement those required by the SVL, and are discussed in Chapter 9.

Others argue that the current SVL be scrapped and replaced by dynamic valuations with both assets and liabilities based on market values. A specific solvency margin would then be required, as would a determination of appropriate types and levels of solvency margins. This approach is similar to that used for years in the United Kingdom.

VALUATION STANDARDS IN CANADA

Valuation standards in Canada vary markedly for the period before 1978, the period during which the standard was the 1978 Canadian method (1978-1991), and the PPM period (1992 and thereafter). It is important to note that, unlike in the U.S., each successive standard replaces the previous one. That is, the new standard applies to all in-force policies, not just new policies issued.

Before 1978

Prior to 1978, the prescription of valuation standards in Canada was similar to that in the U.S. A valuation method was acceptable as long as it could be shown to generate reserves not less than those produced by the method specified by law. Maximum interest rates were prescribed, along with several mortality tables, although higher rates of interest or other mortality tables producing weaker reserves could be used with the advance approval of the Superintendent of Insurance. Withdrawal assumptions were not required, but reserves had to be at least equal to cash values for each policy. Deficiency reserves were required for policies where the actual premium receivable was not sufficient to cover the valuation premium.

Like the current situation in the U.S., the one-sided character (reserves could be more conservative, but generally not less conservative) of these requirements was inconsistent with GAAP, as were a number of other accounting practices of life insurance companies. The auditor's report accompanying financial statements generally made it clear that the financial statements had been prepared in accordance with accounting principles prescribed by the Superintendent. Moreover, rapidly rising interest rates prompted an increasing number of individual requests to the Superintendent for approval of valuation interest assumptions greater than the maximum rates set by law.

1978 Canadian Method

Changes in the Canadian and British Insurance Companies Act (the Act) in effect for the period 1978 to 1991 placed the responsibility for policy valuation on the valuation actuary appointed by the directors of the company and recognized as such in the Act. The mandated mortality bases and maximum interest rates were removed and the valuation actuary could use any assumption considered "appropriate to the circumstances" and acceptable to the Superintendent. Any valuation method was permitted provided it produced a reserve not less, for any policy at any duration, than that produced by a method specified in the Act.

In contrast to the previous Act, the assumptions were a two-sided matter: to be appropriate, margins could be neither too large nor too small. The method, however, remained one-sided: there was no statutory upper limit to the safety that could be built into the valuation method.

The method specified in the Act was a modified net premium method in which the initial acquisition cost that could have been deferred (equal to the total present value at date of issue of the excess of all renewal valuation premiums over all renewal net level premiums) was limited to the lesser of 150% of the net level premium or the actual costs incurred "in connection with the issuance of the policy." The total valuation premium for benefits and for amortization of this deferred acquisition cost could not exceed the premium specified in the policy less future administration expenses and dividend expectations. This eliminated the possibility of a deficiency in the policy premium relative to the valuation premium, so that separate deficiency reserves were not required.

The valuation actuary could have taken withdrawals into account either by using withdrawal assumptions or by substituting cash values any time they exceeded reserves. In the former case, the total of all negative reserves and the total of all excesses of cash value over reserve had to be reported. The Superintendent required these amounts to be appropriated from retained earnings, along with certain other amounts.

A reserve also had to be calculated (an estimate was acceptable) by the net level premium method and the annual statement required by the Department of Insurance called for reserves determined by both methods to be shown. The difference (if any) represented the "deferred policy acquisition expenses" to be shown in the statement (Analysis of Liabilities) by deduction from the net level premium reserve to arrive at the reserve determined by the valuation actuary. If the valuation actuary did not use the method specified in the Act, the reserve determined by that method had to be shown in the balance sheet by a footnote. In addition, the reserve increase determined by the specified method had to be shown in the statement of operations and the adjustment to arrive at the increase determined by the method used by the valuation actuary was shown separately.

The company's published financial statements had to include the same reserve as in the annual statement to the Superintendent (after deduction of acquisition expenses), making the financial information from the two statements consistent. The auditor, in reporting on the financial results, could accept the reserve reported by the valuation actuary as presenting fairly the obligations of the company in respect of policies.

Policy Premium Method (PPM)

Neither the 1978 Canadian Method nor the Net Level Premium Method conformed to generally accepted accounting principles. Considerable effort has been directed since 1978 by both the Canadian Institute of Actuaries and the Canadian Institute of Chartered Accountants to bring statutory valuation requirements into line with GAAP. To that end, the Superintendent of Financial Institutions has endorsed the Policy Premium Method (PPM).

"Net" valuation methods are net with respect to expenses. Net methods tend to generate conservative reserves, since expenses are greater in the early policy years and are covered by the expense component of premiums spread over the full premium period. After the premium period, the method is not conservative enough unless future administrative expenses are provided for in some manner.

Modified reserve methods tend to reduce the conservatism of the Net Level Premium Method by providing for amortization of certain acquisition expenses over the premium period. This is done by means of a modification of the net level premium to permit a greater proportion of the policy (gross) premium to be recognized in the valuation. There is usually an arbitrary limit on the amount of modification permitted, as is the case with both CRVM and the 1978 Canadian Method. If the valuation premium exceeds the policy premium a deficiency reserve must be held for the present value of the excess.

The Policy Premium Method treats expenses explicitly and, hence, does not belong to the family of net methods referred to above, but rather is a gross premium valuation method. The method recognizes all expenses expected to be incurred in the future along with all future policy obligations. Similarly, the premiums used in the valuation are the actual gross premiums collectable in the future under the policy. The Policy Premium Method thereby eliminates the following three aspects of net methods that do not conform to GAAP:

(1) The over-provision resulting from anticipating less than the full amount of future premiums.
(2) The under-provision resulting from ignoring future expenses when there are no future premiums to cover them.
(3) The arbitrary upper limit on modifications.

Under PPM the actuary makes an explicit assumption about each contingency that could materially affect the policy liabilities, each assumption consisting of a combination of an expected component and a margin referred to as the *provision for adverse deviation* (PAD). The Canadian Institute of Actuaries has published standards with respect to the selection of valuation margins for non-par insurance products. It should be noted that unlike U.S. GAAP, actuarial assumptions for traditional products under the Policy Premium Method are not fixed at the time of policy issue, but must be reviewed in light of emerging experience or actuarial judgement.

Valuation Assumptions

In 1979, the Canadian Institute of Actuaries issued its Recommendations for Life Insurance Company Financial Reporting, governing, among other things, the development of appropriate valuation assumptions. The Recommendations incorporate the following general principles regarding assumptions:

(1) An appropriate assumption is required for each contingency that materially affects the company's net income for the policies over their lifetime.
(2) Each assumption should include a contingency margin, thereby increasing the actuarial liability, but the combined effect of all margins should be reasonable.
(3) Larger margins should be used where there is greater uncertainty.

(4) Greater care should be taken in setting assumptions regarding contingencies to which the actuarial liabilities are more sensitive.

(5) Provision should not be made for abnormal adverse deviations from expected experience, for catastrophic events, or for major unexpected alterations in mortality or morbidity.

Excluding the margins, valuation assumptions should represent rates of interest and contingencies expected in the future without bias in either direction. Therefore, the use of valuation assumptions prepared in accordance with these Recommendations in combination with the Policy Premium Method of valuation, which has no inherent conservatism, will have the effect of generating expected income each year that is determined by the margins released during the year. This will be the actual case if experience during the year exactly follows the assumptions without the margins. Actual income will fluctuate around the expected amount according to how actual experience compares with the assumptions excluding the margins. It is clear that a company can expect to earn more in respect of those contingencies that involve a greater degree of uncertainty, which is a desired result.

For actuarial liabilities to result in a fair presentation of net income during the year, the Recommendations must be consistently applied at the beginning and end of the year relative to valuation assumptions. This means that if there is a material change during the year in expectations regarding a contingency, the assumption relating to that contingency should be changed accordingly. This will result in a higher or lower actuarial liability and the difference will affect income for the year. The change properly reflects the financial effect on the company of the changes in the contingency that were recognized during the year.

With policy valuations conforming to GAAP under PPM, the CIA has been reviewing its Recommendations (which provide general guidance) and the Valuation Technique Papers (which provide more specific guidelines) to ensure they continue to be applicable. In particular, guidance will be provided for determining valuation assumptions together with the provisions for adverse deviation.

EXERCISES

1. Prove that if EA' is defined as $P_x^{NL} - \alpha_x^{MOD}$, then

$$V^{MOD} = V^{NL} - EA'\left(\frac{\ddot{a}_{x+t}}{a_x}\right).$$

2. What is the formula for the reserve net premiums for a whole life plan with reserves that are CRVM through the end of year five, grading to net level reserves at year twenty?

3. Contrast the Policy Premium Method with the CRVM.

CHAPTER THREE

TYPES OF RESERVE FACTORS

Chapter 2 discussed basic reserve requirements and developed formulas for terminal reserve factors. However, any real valuation involves policies issued throughout the year, so that terminal reserve factors, calculated as of the end of a policy year, are appropriate for only a small number of policies. This chapter looks at methods used in practice to handle this complication, and also considers a number of alternative types of reserve factors in common use.

MEAN AND MID-TERMINAL RESERVES, AND THEIR RELATIONSHIP TO DEFERRED AND UNEARNED PREMIUMS

Mean Reserves

Consider an annual premium policy being valued on $12/31/z$. If the policy were issued on $1/1/z-t+1$, the correct reserve liability would be the tth year terminal reserve, discussed in Chapter 2, which, as of the end of the tth policy year, is

$$_tV_x = A_{x+t} - P_x \cdot \ddot{a}_{x+t}. \tag{3.1}$$

If, however, the policy were issued on $12/31/z-t+1$, the correct reserve would be the tth year *initial reserve*, which exists at the beginning of policy year t, and is given by

$$_{t-1}V_x + P_x, \tag{3.2}$$

the terminal reserve at duration $t-1$ plus the net premium. In general, for a policy issued a fraction h of the year from the beginning of year $z-t+1$, the *interpolated mean reserve* is defined by

$$(1 - h) \cdot (_{t-1}V_x + P_x) + h \cdot {}_tV_x. \tag{3.3}$$

To simplify calculations and to make the results easier to check, most companies assume that all policies of a given duration were issued 6 months prior to the date of valuation. This allows the company to calculate the reserves for a group of similar policies issued in year $z-t+1$ as the total face amount for the group times the tth year *mean reserve* factor, which is the mean of the initial and terminal reserves. It is equal to the interpolated mean reserve with $h = \frac{1}{2}$, and is given by

$$_tMV_x = \frac{1}{2}\left(_{t-1}V_x + {}_tV_x + P_x\right) = \frac{1}{2}\left(_{t-1}V_x + {}_tV_x\right) + \frac{1}{2} \cdot P_x. \tag{3.4}$$

Although the discussion in this chapter assumes that the valuation takes place on $12/31/z$, the principles are equally applicable to valuations on other dates. In the event of a valuation as of $6/30/z$, the factor $_tMV_x$ would be applied to all policies in the tth policy year at that point, which would be all policies issued between $7/1/z-t$ and $6/30/z-t+1$.

Deferred Premiums

Suppose, as is typically the case, the block of policies being valued contains a mix of various premium payment modes, such as annual, quarterly, or monthly. One approach would be to apply the above factors only to the annual mode policies, and to develop separate factors for each other mode. However, to simplify calculations, companies using the above methods almost universally apply the factors based on annual premiums to the entire block, and then make adjustments for the policies using other modes.

$_tMV_x$ is developed by assuming that the entire premium for policy year t was paid at the beginning of that policy year. In reality, for a policy on monthly mode, the mean reserve factor is overstated by the amount of monthly net premiums for policy year t that have not yet become due. *Deferred premiums* are modal premiums that are due after the valuation date but before the next policy anniversary. Deferred premiums are set up either as an asset (in the U.S.) or a negative liability (in Canada) to adjust for the fact that mean reserves based on an annual net premium payment at the beginning of the policy year overstate reserves in the case of more frequent modes of premium payment.[1]

The usual practice is to determine deferred premiums by taking an inventory of the policy premium payment records, and to set up a deferred premium based on the exact number of modal premiums not yet due for each individual policy. The deferred premiums used must be net premiums, because the mean reserves are based on net premiums.

Although deferred premiums are in practice determined by taking a policy inventory, it would be possible to calculate a theoretical average deferred premium assuming that premiums are payable m times per year and that issues are distributed uniformly throughout the year. In this case the average deferred premium is

$$\frac{m-1}{2m} \cdot P_x, \tag{3.5}$$

and the net liability (mean reserve less net deferred premium) is

$$\frac{1}{2}\left({}_{t-1}V_x + {}_tV_x\right) + \frac{1}{2m} \cdot P_x. \tag{3.6}$$

Mid-Terminal Reserves and Unearned Premiums

Instead of mean reserves with deferred premiums, many companies use basic reserve factors based on an alternative approach. Again, assuming a valuation as of $12/31/z$, the *interpolated terminal reserve* for a policy issued a fraction h of the year from the beginning of year $z - t + 1$ is defined as

$$(1 - h) \cdot {}_{t-1}V_x + h \cdot {}_tV_x. \tag{3.7}$$

Although some companies use this approach, it is generally assumed once again that all policies of a given duration were issued 6 months prior to the date of valuation. We then define the tth year *mid-terminal reserve* to be

---

[1] Uncollected premiums, on the other hand, are premiums that have fallen due on or before the valuation date but have not yet been paid.

$$\frac{1}{2}\left(_{t-1}V_x + _tV_x\right). \tag{3.8}$$

It has been common practice to use mean reserve factors for ordinary business, and mid-terminal factors for weekly premium industrial and long-term disability. However, a number of companies use mid-terminal factors for ordinary business.

Mid-terminal reserves understate the reserve liability unless premiums are payable very frequently, such as weekly. This can be seen by comparing the mid-terminal reserve formula (3.8) to the mean reserve formula (3.4). The mean reserve exceeds the mid-terminal by $\frac{1}{2}P_x$, yet we had previously determined that the mean reserve is appropriate for annual premium policies.

To offset this understatement, an *unearned premium liability* is set up as an adjustment. The unearned premium liability is, in practice, calculated on either a gross or net basis; however, most companies calculate unearned premiums for ordinary life policies on a net basis.

The usual practice is to determine the unearned premium liability by taking one-half of the sum of one modal premium for each policy in force. If the modal premiums are listed by mode and latest month paid, the actual number of months unearned can be reflected.

Theoretically the total net liability using mean reserves (mean reserve less deferred premium) is equal to that using mid-terminal reserves (midterminal reserve plus unearned premium) under the assumption of uniform distribution of issues. In this case, assuming premiums are payable m times per year, the unearned premium is

$$\frac{1}{2m} \cdot P_x, \tag{3.9}$$

and the net liability in either case is given by formula (3.6) above.

GRAPHIC REPRESENTATION OF RESERVES

Relationships between mean and mid-terminal reserves may be seen more clearly through diagrams such as Figures 3.1 and 3.2 on pages 39 and 40, for a policy issued on June 30.

In these diagrams, the thin line indicates the interpolated "mean" reserves, and the dashed line represents interpolated (or "mid") terminals.

The important points on the line include

(1) the mean reserve at year-end $z - 1$,
(2) the mid-terminal reserve at year-end $z - 1$,
(3) the terminal reserve for policy year $t - 1$, and
(4) the initial reserve for policy year t.

If the policy were on an *annual* mode basis at year-end $z - 1$, then there would be no deferred premium asset, and point (1) would represent the net liability assuming mean reserves. In this case, if mid-terminals were used, the unearned net premium would equal one half of the annual net premium, which is the difference between (1) and (2). Thus, the net liability assuming mid-terminal reserves is again point (1).

FIGURE 3.1

Anniversary:

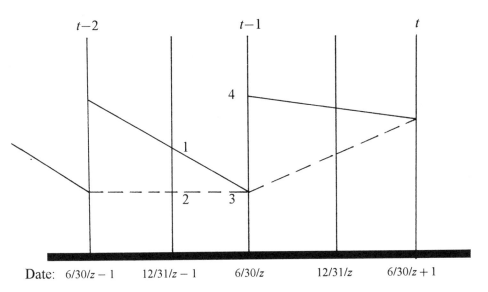

Date: $6/30/z - 1$ $12/31/z - 1$ $6/30/z$ $12/31/z$ $6/30/z + 1$

Now assume that the policy is actually *quarterly* mode rather than annual, and that the quarterly premium was paid December 31; this case is illustrated in Figure 3.2.

The thin and dashed lines, reproduced from Figure 3.1, assume annual payment of premiums, in line with typical curtate mechanics. The boldest line indicates the net liability for a quarterly mode policy. Thus (1) – (5) is the

amount of the net deferred premium assuming mean reserves are held, and
(5) − (2) is the amount of the net unearned premium assuming mid-terminals.
Once again, we see that the net liability is independent of the type of reserve
held.

FIGURE 3.2

Anniversary:

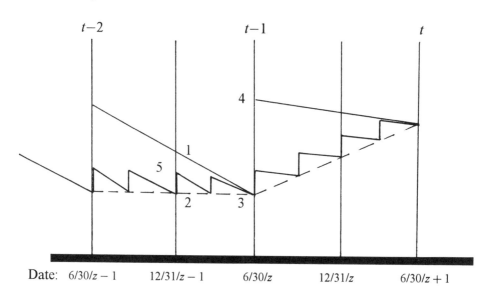

OTHER RESERVE ADJUSTMENTS AND
ALTERNATIVE TYPES OF FACTORS

Curtate and Semicontinuous Factors

Prior formulas implied the use of curtate functions, which are based on the
assumptions that (a) annual net premiums are payable at the beginning of each
policy year, and (b) death benefits are payable at the end of the policy year of
death. In practice, most companies use *curtate reserves* for their basic reserve factors.

Although the assumption as to annual payment of premiums may be
accurate in a particular situation, the two assumptions which define curtate reserves are made primarily in order to simplify calculations. In particular, the

assumption that death benefits are payable at the end of the policy year of death has no basis in fact for modern life insurance contracts, and is made to make the formulas simpler, which was a primary consideration before the computer age. Curtate reserves are so widely used that it is a common misbelief of actuaries and nonactuaries alike that "standard actuarial practice" is to assume that annual premiums are payable at the beginning of the year and death benefits at the end. However, in many situations these may be inappropriate, non-actuarial assumptions. In particular, when performing a realistic model office projection, as in the case of an appraisal valuation or a financial projection, it is never appropriate to assume deaths at year-end.

Because death benefits are actually paid near the time of death instead of at the end of the year, an additional reserve, the *immediate payment of claims reserve*, is traditionally held in addition to the basic curtate reserve. The immediate payment of claims reserve is often developed using relatively crude techniques. Actuarial Guideline XXXII requires that an immediate payment of claims reserve be established, if the basic reserves have been calculated using curtate factors:

- If the policy contract calls for payment of interest on the death proceeds from the date of death to the date of payment, AG XXXII requires an IPC reserve of $\frac{i}{2}$ times the death portion of the basic reserve (i.e. $A^1_{x:\overline{n}|}$ for an *n*-year endowment contract).
- If the contract provides for payment of death claims immediately upon receipt of due proof of death, without interest from the date of death, AG XXXII requires an IPC reserve of $\frac{i}{3}$ times the death portion of the basic reserve.
- No IPC reserve is required for policies which provide for payment of death claims at the end of the policy year of death, or if the basic reserve factors are semicontinuous, fully continuous or discounted continuous.

Semicontinuous reserves are explicitly calculated under the assumption that death benefits are payable at the moment of death and that net premiums are payable annually at the beginning of the year. A number of companies use this basis for their basic reserve factors, eliminating the need for immediate payment of claims reserves.

The net premium for semicontinuous reserves is

$$P(\bar{A}_x) = \frac{\bar{A}_x}{\ddot{a}_x}, \tag{3.10}$$

and the terminal reserve is

$$_tV(\bar{A}_x) = \bar{A}_{x+t} - P(\bar{A}_x) \cdot \ddot{a}_{x+t}. \tag{3.11}$$

Fully Continuous and Discounted Continuous Factors

Fully continuous reserves are those which would result from the assumption that premiums are payable continuously throughout the year and death benefits are payable at the moment of death. Again, the assumption that premiums are payable continuously throughout the year has been made for the sake of convenience only, and does not necessarily have a basis in fact,[2] as continuous reserves may be used for policies with any mode of premium payment. The assumption that death benefits are payable at the moment of death does, however, accurately reflect modern policies. No immediate payment of claims reserve is needed if the basic reserve factors are fully continuous. Note that since premiums are assumed to be payable continuously throughout the year, mean reserves cannot really be used under continuous assumptions.

Fully continuous reserves have largely given way in practice to *discounted continuous reserves*, which are also calculated on the assumption that death benefits are payable at the moment of death. Net premiums are assumed to be payable annually at the beginning of the year with a refund of the unearned portion of the current year's premium at death. Terminal reserves are identical to those on a fully continuous basis. Thus, in practice, the net premium used in calculating terminal reserves for a whole life policy is

$$\bar{P}(\bar{A}) = \frac{\bar{A}_x}{\ddot{a}_x}. \tag{3.12}$$

However, mean reserves reflect the discounted continuous premium payable at the beginning of the year (discounted with interest only). For a whole life policy, the amount payable at the beginning of the year is[3]

---

[2] Although for weekly premium industrial insurance it is not an unreasonable assumption. Continuous reserves have sometimes been used for such policies.

[3] Discounted continuous reserves can be viewed as having two net premiums: one used to calculate terminal reserves, and another to calculate mean reserves.

$$\overline{a}_{\overline{1}|} \cdot \overline{P}(\overline{A}_x) = \overline{a}_{\overline{1}|} \left(\frac{\overline{A}_x}{\overline{a}_x} \right). \tag{3.13}$$

Discounted continuous reserves are often calculated using traditional curtate reserve mechanics, including a deferred premium asset to adjust for modes other than annual.

Discounted continuous reserves are in widespread use as most companies which hold "continuous reserves" actually use this method. This is because the assumption that premiums are paid annually at the beginning of the policy year enables the use of traditional mean reserve methodology and computer systems, and also because the Society of Actuaries has published continuous monetary values using this technique.

The differences between fully continuous and discounted continuous reserves can be summarized as follows:

(1) Fully continuous reserves are based on net premiums payable continuously throughout the year. Reserve factors are midterminals and an unearned premium reserve must be set up for net premiums paid beyond the valuation date.

(2) Discounted continuous terminal reserves are equal to fully continuous terminals. However, mean reserves are calculated assuming an annual net premium equal to the continuous net premium discounted with interest only. A deferred premium asset is calculated if the mode is other than annual.

Table 3.1 on page 46 illustrates formulas for net level premiums and reserves under the four methods discussed above. It is relatively easy to derive the formulas for CRVM reserves, based on the choice of the appropriate expense allowance as discussed above. For more information, the paper "Relationships among the Fully Continuous, the Discounted Continuous, and the Semicontinuous Reserve Bases for Ordinary Life Insurance" by Edward Scher in *Transactions XXVI, Part I* is an excellent source.

The Relationship of the Expense Allowance
to the Type of Reserve Factor

Larger net premiums are produced with the semicontinuous and the two continuous methods than with curtate assumptions. Because the expense allowance under the Standard Valuation Law, $P_{x+1} - c_x$, is a function of the renewal net premium for the contract, these methods would generate a larger expense allowance than curtate methods. Whether these larger expense allowances should be permitted under the Standard Valuation Law used to be a matter of some controversy, since the Society of Actuaries had published monetary values for discounted continuous reserves based on curtate expense allowances. Thus, the formula for the published CRVM discounted continuous renewal premium for a whole life policy was

$$\bar{a}_{\overline{1}|} \cdot P(\bar{A}_x) + \left(\frac{P_{x+1} - c_x}{\ddot{a}_x} \right), \tag{3.14}$$

rather than

$$\bar{a}_{\overline{1}|} \cdot \bar{P}(\bar{A}_{x+1}), \tag{3.15}$$

which would result from strict application of preliminary term methodology. Note that the numerator in (3.14), $P_{x+1} - c_x$, is the curtate expense allowance.

In December 1986 the NAIC adopted Actuarial Guideline XVIII, which allows use of expense allowances calculated on the same basis as the reserves. Therefore $\bar{a}_{\overline{1}|} \cdot \bar{P}(\bar{A}_{x+1})$ is the proper renewal premium in the example above.

Nondeduction Reserve

When curtate or semicontinuous reserves are held, a theoretical error is introduced in the basic reserve calculation, which assumes that full annual premiums will be collected each year. This is because the remaining modal premiums will not be collected in the year of death.[4] It is customary to provide for this understatement by setting up a reserve for the nondeduction of deferred fractional premiums at death, more simply called the *nondeduction reserve.* This reserve is, in theory, equal to that for term insurance of an amount equal to the average number of remaining deferred premiums at the date of death under the policy. For an *n*-year endowment policy, the terminal reserve for this amount is

---

[4] Many years ago it was common for companies to subtract the remaining modal premiums from the death benefit.

$$_tV^1_{x:\overline{n|}} \left(\frac{m-1}{2m} \cdot P^{(m)}_{x:\overline{n|}} \right).$$ (3.16)

Refund Reserve

It is common practice for many companies to refund the amount of any gross premiums at death which represents payment for periods beyond the date of death. The reasoning behind this practice is to avoid "penalizing" the policy-holder who could have switched to a more frequent mode just prior to the date of death and paid less for coverage in that year. For policies with this provision, the terminal reserve factor to cover both the refund of premium provision and the nondeduction of deferred premiums is

$$\frac{1}{2} \cdot P^{\{m\}}_{x:\overline{n|}} \cdot _tV^1_{x:\overline{n|}},$$ (3.17)

where

$$P^{\{m\}}_{x:\overline{n|}} \approx \frac{P_{x:\overline{n|}}}{1 - \frac{m-1}{2m} \cdot d - \frac{1}{2} \cdot P_{x:\overline{n|}}}$$ (3.18)

and $d = \frac{i}{1+i}$ is the familiar rate of discount. Note that, except for the term $\frac{m-1}{2m} \cdot d$ in the denominator, formula (3.18) does not depend on the mode of premiums. In practice, this term is often omitted so that the reserve factor can be applied to the entire group of policies, regardless of mode of premium payment.

Fully continuous factors (and discounted continuous factors) already make allowance for nondeduction of premiums and refund of premium at death, so that it is not necessary to establish these additional liabilities.

Table 3.2 on page 47 illustrates which of the miscellaneous liabilities discussed above are needed for a traditional product with both nondeduction of deferred fractional premium at death and a refund of premium feature, under various assumptions as to the primary reserve basis.

TABLE 3.1

COMPARISON OF WHOLE LIFE NET PREMIUMS AND TERMINAL RESERVES FOR PRIMARY RESERVE BASES

Type	Net Premium	Terminal Reserve	Mean Reserve
Curtate	$P_x = \dfrac{A_x}{\ddot{a}_x}$	$_tV_x = A_{x+t} - P_x \cdot \ddot{a}_{x+t}$	$\frac{1}{2}(_{t-1}V_x + _tV_x + P_x)$
Fully Continuous	$\overline{P}(\overline{A}_x) = \dfrac{\overline{A}_x}{\overline{a}_x}$	$_t\overline{V}(\overline{A}_x) = \overline{A}_{x+t} - \overline{P}(\overline{A}_x) \cdot \overline{a}_{x+t}$	$\frac{1}{2}[_{t-1}\overline{V}(\overline{A}_x) + _t\overline{V}(\overline{A}_x)]$
Discounted Continuous	$\overline{P}(\overline{A}_x)$ used in calculating terminal reserves. $\overline{a}_{\overline{1}|} \cdot \overline{P}(\overline{A}_x)$ used in calculating mean reserves.	$_t\overline{V}(\overline{A}_x) = \overline{A}_{x+t} - \overline{P}(\overline{A}_x) \cdot \overline{a}_{x+t}$	$\frac{1}{2}[_{t-1}\overline{V}(\overline{A}_x) + _t\overline{V}(\overline{A}_x) + \overline{a}_{\overline{1}|} \cdot \overline{P}(\overline{A}_x)]$
Semi-continuous	$P(\overline{A}_x) = \dfrac{\overline{A}_x}{\ddot{a}_x}$	$_tV(\overline{A}_x) = \overline{A}_{x+t} - P(\overline{A}_x) \cdot \ddot{a}_{x+t}$	$\frac{1}{2}[_{t-1}V(\overline{A}_x) + _tV(\overline{A}_x) + P(\overline{A}_x)]$

Note: Arguable, mean reserves are not applicable in the fully continuous case.

TABLE 3.2

NECESSARY MISCELLANEOUS LIABILITIES UNDER PRIMARY RESERVE BASES

Type	Refund Reserve	Nondeduction Reserve	Immediate Payment of Claims Reserve	Deferred Premiums		Unearned Premiums	
				If Mean	If Mid-Terminal	If Mean	If Mid-Terminal
Curtate	Yes	Yes	Yes	Yes	No	No	Yes
Fully Continuous	No	No	No	N/A	No	N/A	Yes
Discounted Continuous	No	No	No	Yes	N/A	No	N/A
Semi-continuous	Yes	Yes	No	Yes	No	No	Yes

Note: Above assumes policy has both nondeduction of deferred premiums and refund of unearned premium at death as policy provisions.

EXERCISES

1. Formulas (3.5) and (3.6) give the deferred premium and net liability under the assumption of uniform distribution of issues. Give the values of these items at year end for a monthly mode policy under the assumption that the issue date is March 1, using each of the following:

   (a) Mean reserves
   (b) Discounted continuous mean reserves

2. If a company's basic reserve factors have been developed by assuming premiums paid continuously and death benefits at the end of the year of death, which of the following would be held as an additional reserve?

   (a) Refund reserve
   (b) Nondeduction reserve
   (c) Immediate payment of claims reserve

3. Describe how fully continuous and discounted continuous reserves differ.

4. For a 20-pay-life contract with premiums payable monthly, what is the terminal reserve at time t $(t < 20)$ for nondeduction of deferred fractional premiums?

CHAPTER FOUR

VALUATION OF INTEREST-SENSITIVE LIFE PRODUCTS

Traditional life insurance products generally provide a guaranteed set of future cash values and death benefits for a stated premium. Even participating products are easily valued using traditional valuation techniques since dividends are typically paid in cash, used to buy additional term coverage, used to buy paid-up additions, or used to pay premiums. In any event, dividends do not affect the basic coverage guaranteed by the terms of the contract.

The interest-sensitive products sold in the U.S. today develop surrender cash values that are based on a retrospective accumulation of premiums (which may be flexible) less mortality and expense charges, at a rate of interest declared by the company or based upon some index. These features are not compatible with the valuation procedures used for traditional products.

FLEXIBLE PREMIUM UNIVERSAL LIFE

Universal Life is an interest-sensitive life insurance product which typically has a "fund." Premiums less expense charges are credited to the fund, along with periodic interest credits, and mortality and expense charges are regularly deducted. The cash value, which is the amount available to the policyholder upon termination of the contract, may be equal to the fund, or it may be equal to the fund less a surrender charge. Flexible Premium Universal Life is a contract for which the policyholder has some degree of flexibility as to the timing or amount of one or more premium payments.[1] Flexible premium products introduce special valuation problems in that some assumption as to future premiums is required.

The typical "present value of future benefits less the present value of future net premiums" formula is impossible to apply to flexible premium universal life policies since neither "future premiums" nor "future benefits" are known for any particular policy.

Many of the early companies to sell universal life (UL) policies used the following rationale for holding the cash surrender value as a reserve:

(1) The cash value formula was the monthly equivalent of a retrospective reserve formula.

(2) The product was sold as permanent coverage. Policyholders could, of course, develop many different benefit patterns depending on their level of contributions.

(3) First year expense or surrender charges were typically less than the CRVM expense allowance for permanent plans.

Other early entrants to the UL market argued that at any point in time, the product could be thought of as a paid-up policy, since no future premiums were required. On this basis, for front-loaded products, the cash value was argued to be a proper reserve for future guaranteed benefits if policy guarantees of mortality and interest were identical to the valuation basis.

However, as products were developed which incorporated back-end loads assessed only on surrender, it became a matter of some controversy as to whether the policy fund accumulation, the cash surrender value (net of surrender charges), or some intermediate value would be the appropriate reserve.

Minimum Reserves

In December of 1983, the NAIC promulgated a model regulation that sets forth a minimum reserving method for UL products. The rules in this regulation represent an effort to fit UL into traditional valuation methodologies. An assumption was made regarding future premium payments and a factor was developed to adjust for actual policy performance.

---

[1] According to New York Regulation 147, "a universal life insurance policy which permits the policyholder to vary, independently of each other, the amount or timing of one or more premium payments."

To calculate CRVM reserves for flexible premium UL products under this regulation the following are necessary:

(1) A *Guaranteed Maturity Premium* (GMP) is calculated. The GMP is the level gross premium that provides for an endowment at the latest permissible maturity date under the contract. As its name implies, the GMP is calculated as of the issue date[2] using policy guarantees as to expense charges, mortality charges, and interest credits.

(2) A set of *Guaranteed Maturity Funds* (GMF's) must be calculated. GMF's are the fund values calculated as of the issue date[3] using policy guarantees and assuming that GMP's are paid.

(3) The actual fund value at the valuation date must be known.

(4) The ratio, r, of the actual fund value to the GMF is calculated. r is never allowed to exceed 1.

(5) The policy fund is projected forward from the valuation date, on a guaranteed basis, using the larger of the actual fund or the GMF, and assuming that GMP's are paid. This projection produces a set of "guaranteed death benefits" and a "guaranteed maturity benefit" for valuation purposes.[4] The present value of these benefits is calculated on the valuation basis.

(6) A net level reserve is calculated as r times the difference between the present value of future benefits, described above, and the present value of net level premiums. These net level premiums are calculated based on the plan of insurance produced at issue on a guaranteed basis assuming GMP's are paid. (Using the same technique as described above, but calculated as of the issue date rather than the valuation date.)

(7) The CRVM reserve is calculated as the difference between the net level reserve determined above and r times the unamortized CRVM expense allowance for the plan of insurance generated at issue on a guaranteed basis and assuming GMP's are paid.

---

[2] The GMP is recalculated if the policyholder initiates a change in the benefit structure of the policy.

[3] The GMFs are recalculated if the policyholder initiates a change in the benefit structure of the policy.

[4] UL policies typically contain cash value corridors such that the death benefit at an attained age is at least equal to the policy fund times the applicable corridor percent. Depending upon the level of the policy fund at the valuation date, this can result in guaranteed death benefits exceeding those which would otherwise be payable.

In essence, the model regulation assumes that at issue, all UL policies are permanent plans. The r factor is meant to measure whether or not the policy is "on track" as a permanent plan.

As with reserves for all life policies in the U.S., any excess of the cash value of the policy over the reserve must be held as a liability in Exhibit 8, Paragraph G of the NAIC Blank.

Alternative Minimum Reserves

Alternative minimum reserves (AMR's) may be required for flexible premium universal life plans if the GMP is less than the valuation net premium for the plan of insurance produced at issue, on a guaranteed basis, assuming that GMP's are paid.

If the GMP is less than the valuation net premium calculated using minimum standards of mortality and interest, then the reserve held shall be the larger of (a) or (b), defined as

(a) the reserve calculated according to the reserve method, mortality basis, and valuation interest rate actually used for the policy, and

(b) the reserve calculated by the reserve method actually used for the policy but using the minimum standards of mortality and interest allowable for deficiency reserves and replacing the valuation net premium by the GMP.

Following the UL Model Regulation precisely, one discovers that, unlike for traditional insurance plans, the expense deferral portion of the valuation net premium has been dealt with separately by referring to an unamortized expense allowance and a net level premium separately. Thus, the "valuation net premium" referred to above is not explicitly defined in the UL Model Regulation.

It is the interpretation of most companies that a valuation net premium should be calculated for the purpose of calculating AMR's as

$$VNP = P^{NL} + \frac{EA}{\ddot{a}}, \qquad (4.1)$$

where P^{NL} is a net level premium and EA is the initial expense deferral.

Product features that lead to AMR's include the following:

(1) No-load products can develop AMR's if the guaranteed cost bases of mortality charges and interest is very similar to the valuation basis.

(2) Guaranteed cost of insurance rates that are lower than valuation mortality can lead to AMR's, especially if the guaranteed interest rate equals the valuation interest rate and the level of front-end loads is fairly low.

(3) Guaranteed interest rates in excess of the valuation rate can lead to AMR's, especially if the guaranteed cost of insurance rates equal the valuation mortality and the level of loads is fairly low.

(4) Any product feature than tends to lower the GMP creates the potential for AMR's.

Examples Using Flexible Premium Plans

Once the GMP, GMF, and net level premium have been calculated, terminal reserves can be determined for any duration. To review, this is done for duration t by taking the greater of the GMF at duration t and the actual fund for the individual policy being valued, and accumulating the policy values forward until the maturity date, assuming payment each year of the GMP. In order to calculate net level reserves for the policy, the present value of the resulting death benefits and maturity values is determined as of duration t.

This present value is determined by using the valuation basis of interest and mortality. The net level reserve at duration t is r times the result of taking the present value of future benefits minus the present value of future net level premiums, where r is the ratio of the actual fund value to the guaranteed maturity fund at duration t. Mathematically this is

$$_t V^{NL} = r(PVFB_t - P^{NL} \cdot \ddot{a}_{x+t}), \qquad (4.2)$$

where $PVFB_t$ is the present value on the valuation basis of future benefits at duration t, based on a projection of the policy fund values using the policy guarantees, starting with the greater of the actual fund and GMF, and assuming payment of GMP's throughout the remaining premium paying period of the policy; $\ddot{a}_{x+t}$ is an annuity of one per year continuing throughout the remaining premium paying period; and r is the ratio of the actual fund at duration t to GMF_t, not to exceed 1.

To calculate CRVM reserves for the policy, net level reserves are reduced by

$$r \cdot EA^{CRVM} \cdot \frac{\ddot{a}_{x+t}}{\ddot{a}_x}, \tag{4.3}$$

where EA^{CRVM} is the first year CRVM allowance at issue for the plan of insurance defined by the GMP's and all the policy guarantees, and $\ddot{a}_x$ is an annuity, as of the issue date, of one per year continuing throughout the premium paying period. $\ddot{a}_{x+t}$ and r are as defined above.

EXAMPLE A

Consider a typical back-loaded product with a 3% of premium front-end load and a 4% guaranteed interest rate, issued at age 35. (Detailed specifications for all examples are found in Appendix C.) The GMP, the premium at issue necessary to endow for 1,000 at age 95, is 14.49.

A practical problem in calculating reserves arises from the fact that UL accumulations and the resulting guaranteed death benefits typically involve monthly mechanics, whereas present values are traditionally taken on an annual basis. Thus, there is a stream of death benefits varying monthly which are required to be discounted to the valuation date. Several reasonable methods are possible for handling the monthly/annual problems. In these examples, average death benefits for the year are discounted using continuous functions.

Projecting the fund forward at issue on a guaranteed basis and assuming annual payment of the GMP produces level annual death benefits and an endowment amount at 95 equal to the death benefit. Assuming continuous deaths and annual premium payments at 4.5% interest, we get $P^{CRVM} = 13.80$ and $P^{NL} = 13.16$, which are the same as for traditional endowment at 95 plans.

Assume that it is necessary to calculate the 10th year terminal reserve for a policy with a fund of 195.75 at the end of the 10th year. To find the 10th year terminal reserve, it is necessary to calculate GMF_{10} by accumulating the GMP's to the 10th duration on a guaranteed basis. In this example, $GMF_{10} = 136.70$. Because the policy fund is greater than GMF_{10}, r is equal to 1. Next the actual fund is projected on a guaranteed basis to age 95, and the present value of the generated benefits is determined. (For Example A, this calculation is detailed in Appendix C.) This present value comes to $\bar{A} = 381.65$. The present value of future net level premiums is $P^{NL} \cdot \ddot{a}_{45:\overline{50}|} = (13.16)(15.6193) = 205.55$.

Next, the unamortized CRVM allowance is

$$r\left(P^{CRVM} - P^{NL}\right) \cdot \ddot{a}_{45:\overline{50}|}, \tag{4.4}$$

which, in this case, is $(1)(13.80 - 13.16)(15.6193) = 10.00$.
Finally, the terminal reserve based on 4.5% 58 CSO is

$$_{10}V = \bar{A}_{45} - P^{NL} \cdot \ddot{a}_{45:\overline{50}|} - \left(P^{CRVM} - P^{NL}\right) \cdot \ddot{a}_{45:\overline{50}|}, \tag{4.5}$$

which, in this case, yields $381.65 - 205.55 - 10.00 = 166.10$. Notice how much lower this is than the fund balance of 195.75. However, the cash surrender value in this example is 187.99, which would be the total liability.

| EXAMPLE B |

Consider the same product, but with a tenth year fund of 57.74, which is less than GMF_{10}. Now we find $r = \frac{57.75}{136.70} = .4224$.

Projecting GMF_{10} on a guaranteed basis produces a level death benefit of 1,000 and an endowment amount at 95 of 1,000. The present value of future benefits produced by assuming a fund value equal to GMF_{10} is 334.68. The present value of future net premiums and the unamortized expense allowance are unchanged. Therefore the terminal reserve is

$$_{10}V = r\left[\bar{A} - P^{NL} \cdot \ddot{a}_{45:\overline{50}|} - \left(P^{CRVM} - P^{NL}\right) \cdot \ddot{a}_{45:\overline{50}|}\right] \tag{4.6}$$

$$= .4224(334.68 - 205.55 - 10.00) = 50.32.$$

| EXAMPLE C |

The same product, but the 3% front-end load is removed, and the guaranteed interest rate is increased to 4.5%. Alternative minimum reserves should arise. In this case, we get $GMP = 13.04$ and $GMF_{10} = 127.59$.

Assume that the tenth year fund is 177.63. The valuation premiums are unchanged, so

$$P^{CRVM} = P^{NL} + \frac{EA}{\ddot{a}_x} = 13.80 > GMP. \tag{4.7}$$

Assuming the valuation basis is also the one used to calculate deficiency reserves, terminal reserves must be calculated using *GMP* instead of P^{NL} and the expense allowance. The present value of future benefits at duration 10 is 382.69, so the terminal reserve is $382.69 - (13.04)(15.6193) = 179.01$, which is very close to the fund value of 177.63.

⎡ EXAMPLE D ⎤

The same product as Example C, but with a 3% of premium load. A possible way to reduce alternative minimum reserves is to introduce expense loads (which may or may not be charged on a current basis). In Example C, if a 3% load is introduced, everything remains the same except that GMP is now 13.44. Alternative minimum reserves are still required (since P^{CRVM} exceeds P^{GMP}), but are reduced to $382.69 - (13.44)(15.6193) = 172.77$. Alternative minimum reserves could be eliminated entirely if an even larger expense load were imposed.

Note that the above defines terminal net level reserves for the policy. Appropriate adjustments would have to be made in order to calculate mean reserves.

FIXED PREMIUM UNIVERSAL LIFE

Many companies offer products whose cash values are calculated using UL accumulation procedures, but which lack complete flexibility in premium payments. Some of these products also offer the policyholder a "secondary guarantee." Secondary guarantees are discussed in detail later in this chapter.

When these products were first sold, the typical reserving practice was to hold the higher of (a) or (b) as a statutory reserve, defined as

(a) a traditionally calculated CRVM reserve for the plan of insurance provided by the secondary guarantee, and
(b) the actual cash value.

This sort of product fits existing statutory valuation rules and procedures far better than flexible premium UL. At any point in time, the present value of future benefits (PVFB's) can be determined and future premium payments are fixed (although they may be waived through a "vanishing premium" provision).

This product falls under a similar set of valuation rules set out in the NAIC Model Regulation for Universal Life. The key differences in the valuation procedure for fixed premium policies are as follows:

(1) The GMP is equal to the gross premium.
(2) The expense allowance (EA) and the rate of amortization are determined by the plan of insurance guaranteed at issue.[5]
(3) The *r* factor always equals one.

Given these parameters, the procedure to calculate CRVM reserves can be simplified for fixed premium products to the following:

(1) Project future benefits on a guaranteed basis, taking secondary guarantees into account where necessary.
(2) Value the benefits described above using valuation mortality and interest.
(3) Subtract the present value of future CRVM net premiums for the plan of insurance guaranteed at issue.

The necessity to project future benefits based on the actual policy fund value causes these reserves to be cumbersome to calculate, even with computing equipment. However, a product may be constructed such that a projection is not required to ensure that the reserves meet minimum standards. In certain situations described in Appendix D, it is proper to use the early method of holding the greater of a CRVM reserve for the plan guaranteed at issue or the actual cash value.

SECONDARY GUARANTEES

Both fixed and flexible premium Universal Life policies may contain secondary guarantees. A secondary guarantee provides the policyholder a guaran-

---

[5] Including the effect of any secondary guarantees.

teed set of cash values, death benefits and/or maturity benefits that will be provided regardless of the performance of the fund. Examples include:

- A fixed premium UL whose premium is at a level which would not carry the policy to maturity on a guaranteed basis, which provides that, as long as the policyholder keeps paying the level premium, the policy will stay inforce regardless of the performance of the fund (even though the policy generally lapses if the fund goes to zero).
- A flexible premium universal life insurance policy which normally lapses when the fund less the surrender charge is zero, but which provides that, if the policyholder pays a stated minimum premium each of the first ten years, the policy will not lapse during the ten year period, even if the fund less the surrender charge is negative.

In 1995 the NAIC adopted the Valuation of Life Insurance Policies Model Regulation. The Valuation Model Regulation imposes minimum reserve requirements on Universal Life policies that contain secondary guarantees which cause the policy to remain inforce over a period exceeding 5 years, subject only to the payments of specified premiums. In particular, the Valuation Model Regulation requires that reserves for a policy with such a secondary guarantee are at a minimum equal to reserves equal to the form implied by the secondary guarantee.[6] Thus, in the first example above, the reserve would, at a minimum, equal the reserve for a whole life policy, since the policyholder is guaranteed that the policy will stay inforce as long as level premiums are paid. In the second example, the minimum reserve during the first ten years would equal a ten year term reserve. In both cases, the regular reserve required by the Universal Life Model Regulation is to be held, if greater.

---

[6] Technically, the Valuation Model Regulation requires that "basic reserves for the secondary guarantees shall be the segmented reserves (as defined in Chapter 7) for the secondary guarantee period ... Deficiency reserves, if any, for the secondary guarantees shall be calculated for the secondary guarantee period ... with gross premiums set equal to the specified premiums, if any, or otherwise to the minimum premiums that keep the policy in force ... The minimum reserves during the secondary guarantee period are the greater of: (1) the basic reserves for the secondary guarantee plus the deficiency reserve, if any, for the secondary guarantees; or (2) the minimum reserves required by other rules or regulations governing universal life plans."

Off-Anniversary Reserves

The Universal Life Model Regulation defines terminal reserves but is silent on how to calculate off-anniversary reserves. As a consequence, many reasonable methods have been developed and are in current use. The main issues in calculating off-anniversary reserves include the following:

(1) How to calculate r; should r be calculated as of the valuation date, or as of either the prior or next policy anniversary?
(2) How to calculate the GMF on the valuation date in the event r is calculated as of the valuation date.
(3) Whether to calculate the reserve factors from first principles as of the valuation date, or, alternatively, to calculate a mean, mid-terminal, or interpolated reserve.

Although it may not be unreasonable to calculate off-anniversary reserves using an r value calculated as of either the prior or next policy anniversary, it is generally considered to be more accurate to calculate an r value as of the valuation date. This brings up the question of how to calculate the GMF as of the valuation date, and specifically whether to use annual GMP's or GMP's consistent with the policy's planned premium mode. It is important that the choice be consistent with the reserve method used. For example, if the GMF is calculated assuming annual GMP's and mean reserve factors are used, no deferred premiums are required for the policy. If, on the other hand, the GMF is calculated using GMP's based on the planned premium mode for the policy and mean reserve factors are used, then net deferred premiums are required for monthly mode policies. These net deferred premiums should be multiplied by r.

Whether net deferred premiums or unearned premiums are required is based on the assumption inherent in the GMF, not on the actual policy mode. Thus, if the GMF is based on monthly GMP's and mean reserves are used, net deferred premiums are required. Similarly, if the GMF is calculated assuming annual GMP's and mid-terminal reserves are held, unearned premiums must be held.

One advantage of calculating reserve factors from first principles as of the date of valuation is that it is possible to avoid net deferred and unearned premiums. However, the use of mean or mid-terminal reserves may make it easier to check the valuation.

FIGURE 4.1

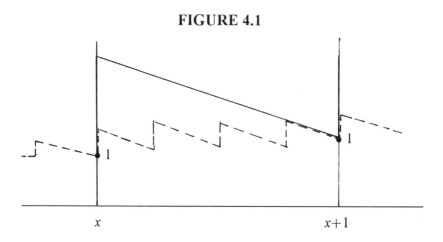

In Figure 4.1, x and $x+1$ are the ages on policy anniversary dates. The dark line represents the GMF assuming annual GMP's. The dotted line represents the GMF assuming quarterly GMP's. Points (1) are the only parts of the graph explicitly defined in the model regulation. Note the similarity between Figure 4.1 and Figure 3.2.

POSSIBLE CHANGES AND THE CALIFORNIA UNIVERSAL LIFE REGULATION

Some actuaries feel that the CRVM for Universal Life is unnecessarily complex and that alternative methods should be investigated. In addition, there is concern that in certain situations, the reserve may be inadequate. The NAIC Actuarial Task Force has exposed different proposals for changing the model regulation, but none of the proposals have been adopted. To some degree, the industry has opposed simplification of the model regulation, since, for existing business, tax reserves for Universal Life are defined in terms of the existing NAIC model regulation. Therefore, some companies felt that for tax reporting purposes they would be forced to calculate universal life reserves using two different methodologies indefinitely into the future.

One method which has received extensive consideration is called the *guaranteed maturity premium method.* This method produces results that are consistent with the existing model regulation. Under the GMP method, the company would still have to calculate guaranteed maturity premiums and guaranteed maturity funds. However, projections as of the valuation date of future guaranteed benefits would be unnecessary. Under the GMP method, the r factor and traditional CRVM reserves would be used to calculate the Universal Life CRVM reserve. The "traditional CVRM reserves" would be those based on a permanent life insurance plan with a maturity at the latest possible maturity date under the universal plan. Then

$$_tV^{GMP\,Method} = r \cdot {}_tV^{CRVM} \tag{4.8a}$$

if $Fund_t \leq GMF_t$, and

$$_tV^{GMP\,Method} = {}_tV^{CRVM} + Fund_t - GMF_t \tag{4.8b}$$

if $Fund_t > GMF_t$. In (4.8a) and (4.8b) $_tV^{CRVM}$ is the traditional CRVM reserve and $Fund_t$ is the actual account value.

For policies where the r factor is less than 1, it can be demonstrated algebraically that this method produces values that will duplicate the model regulation. For policies where the account value is larger than the guaranteed maturity fund, the GMP method was felt to be a reasonable approximation for most products.

In 1991 the California Department of Insurance issued a regulation on Universal Life reserves for policies issued after December 31, 1991. It is similar to the Universal Life model regulation, except that the valuation interest rate may not exceed the credited rate guaranteed in the contract. This causes minimum reserves to be higher than otherwise, since it had been common for companies to guarantee a credited rate such as 4% and to use a valuation rate such as 5.5%.

The California regulation allows companies, at their option, to alternatively hold a reserve equal to the mean of the cash value and the fund value. This method is defined in the regulation as the *California Method*. Note that the California Method may produce reserves greater or less than the model regulation reserves, depending upon the relationship of the fund to the GMF and the contract design. For example, reserves under the California Method would always equal the cash value for a front-end loaded Universal Life plan, and might well be below those required by the model regulation. In 1994 New York adopted Regulation 147, which permits the California method as an elective alternative basis for Universal Life reserves.

As discussed in Chapter 1, since the 1992 valuation actuary opinion under the new Standard Valuation Law requires that reserves be "at least as great as the minimum aggregate amounts required by the state in which this statement is filed," companies filing a California statement will need to take account of this regulation, even if California is not their state of domicile. Also note that since tax reserves are required to be based on the NAIC model regulation, companies opting for the simpler California Method will still be required to calculate model regulation reserves for their tax return.

MINIMUM VERSUS ADEQUATE RESERVES

Use of the cash value as the reserve for flexible premium UL contracts can have the effect of deferring losses to later years. The CRVM for UL as defined by the NAIC, while offering some improvement, may be considered inadequate in some cases, particularly for back-loaded products.

For many UL products with surrender charges, cash values become larger than CRVM reserves once the surrender charges begin to grade off. If UL Model Regulation reserves are used with no modification, renewal losses may occur when the increase in cash value is not supportable by the gross premium. An example of the statutory profit pattern of one such product is given in the following table.

TABLE 4.1

Year	Statutory Book Profit	Present Value of Future Profits
0	-----	.63
1	(2.9930)	3.70
2	5.5280	(1.30)
3	(.2342)	(1.24)
4	(.5100)	(.91)
5	(.6040)	(.44)
6	(1.0136)	.51

As we can see from the column labeled "Present Value of Future Profits," at some durations, the reserve together with future anticipated gross premiums and investment earnings may not be sufficient to provide for expenses and anticipated policyholder benefits. In this scenario, the statutory profits recognized in year two are so large that renewal losses occur as the surrender charge grades off. The plan is profitable at issue, but the statutory reserving basis used recognizes earnings too early. Although this example may not be typical of results obtained by the UL Model Regulation, it illustrates problems that can arise with any product (including traditional life products) whose cash values exceed the reserves.

If a cash surrender value pattern such as this example were to occur in a traditional life insurance policy, the policy would fall under the unusual cash surrender value provision of the Valuation of Life Insurance Model Regulation, which is discussed more fully in Chapter 7. However, the unusual cash surrender value provision is in a section of the Model Regulation which specifically exempts Universal Life insurance.

The results obtained using the UL Model Regulation are very sensitive to the assumed level of investment return. For this reason, testing of more than one scenario may be desirable. A more complete discussion of the asset risk is contained in Chapter 8.

EXERCISES

1. Two Universal Life products, A and B, are identical (i.e., the same loads, policy guarantees, and so on), except that Product A has a 4% valuation rate and Product B has a 5.5% valuation rate. Assume that $100,000 policies of each type are issue on 7/1/87 to age 35 males, and that each has the same fund value as of 12/31/92.

   (a) Which product would have the larger reserve?
   (b) If Product A's fund is exactly equal to its guaranteed maturity fund, describe its reserve (ignoring the cash value floor).
   (c) Assume now that the valuation rates are both 5.5%, but the products differ in that Product A guarantees a 4% fund accumulation and Product B guarantees 5%. Which would have the larger reserve, again assuming identical fund values as of 12/31/92?
   (d) In part (c), which product would have the larger guaranteed maturity fund as of 12/31/92?

2. The following Universal Life products are identical except for the noted items:

Product	Front-end Load	Cost of Insurance Rates	Fund Interest Guarantee
I	0%	100% 75-80 Table	4.0%
II	5%	100% 75-80 Table	4.0
III	5%	100% 75-80 Table	4.5
IV	5%	110% 75-80 Table	4.0

Assuming otherwise identical policies, including identical fund values at the valuation date, which product in each of the following pairs is more likely to require Alternative Minimum Reserves?

(a) I and II   (b) II and III   (c) II and IV

Ignoring Alternative Minimum Reserves, which product in each of the following pairs would produce the larger reserves?

(d) I and II   (e) II and III   (f) II and IV   (g) I and III

3. You are the actuary for a company that sells a Universal Life product which generates Alternative Minimum Reserves. Assume your president wants to eliminate these reserves.

(a) What product features should you consider changing, and how should each be changed (i.e., raised or lowered)?
(b) Will changing the valuation interest rate help?
(c) Will changing the valuation mortality table help?
(d) Will changing the reserve method from net level to CRVM help?

CHAPTER FIVE

VALUATION OF ANNUITIES

Proper statutory reserve methodology in the U.S. for deferred annuities was not clearly defined prior to the 1976 amendments to the Standard Valuation Law. Historically, annuities had been a relatively unimportant part of the life insurance industry, primarily used to provide a guaranteed income stream after retirement. However, with the dramatic increase in interest rates in the 1970's, more and more companies began to sell single and flexible premium deferred annuities designed to serve primarily as cash accumulation vehicles. With the increase in annuity reserves in the 1970's,[1] the NAIC felt it necessary to formalize the basis of minimum reserves for such policies. As a result, the *Commissioners Annuity Reserve Valuation Method* (CARVM) was developed.

The 1976 amendments define CARVM in the following paragraph:

> "Reserves according to the commissioners annuity reserve method for benefits under annuity or pure endowment contracts, excluding any disability and accidental death benefits in such contracts, shall be the greatest of the respective excesses of the present values, at the date of valuation, of the future guaranteed benefits, including guaranteed non-forfeiture benefits, provided for by such contracts at the end of each respective contract year, over the present value, at the date of valuation, of any future valuation considerations derived from future gross

---

[1] In 1982 total annuity reserves of U.S. life companies exceeded life reserves for the first time in history (see graph on page 66).

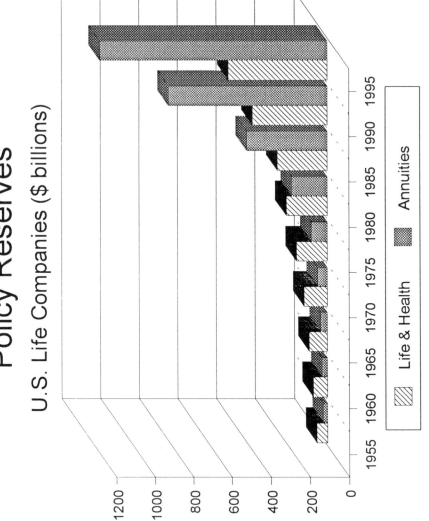

considerations, required by the terms of such contract, that become payable prior to the end of such respective contract year. The future guaranteed benefits shall be determined by using the mortality table, if any, and the interest rate, or rates, specified in such contracts for determining guaranteed benefits. The valuation considerations are the portions of the respective gross considerations applied under the terms of such contracts to determine nonforfeiture values."[2]

CARVM defines the minimum U.S. standard for individual annuities, and also for group annuities that are issued neither to a qualified pension plan nor to an Individual Retirement Account.

After adoption of CARVM as the standard annuity reserve valuation method, many life insurance companies were slow to implement CARVM, at least partly due to its perceived complexity. Instead, many companies continued to hold more conservative reserves which were easier to calculate. However, with the adoption of CARVM as the required methodology for calculation of Federally Prescribed Tax Reserves (FPTR's), companies have been forced to implement this reserve technique.

The remainder of this section will examine how CARVM works and will look at problems that may arise in applying CARVM to common annuity designs. For questions which arise in practice, excellent sources are the NAIC *Proceedings* as well as Jay Jaffe's paper in the *Transactions*[3] and the subsequent discussion. Also, Actuarial Guidelines XXXIII was adopted by the NAIC in 1995 to address several outstanding CARVM issues. However, it should be noted that there is still disagreement over how CARVM applies in many specific cases.

BASIC APPLICATION OF CARVM TO SINGLE PREMIUM DEFERRED ANNUITIES (SPDA's)

Looking at the definition of CARVM above, we see that it is necessary to first project the annuity fund balance forward at the guaranteed basis in the policy, and then to use the projected fund balance to calculate the future guaranteed benefits under the policy. These guaranteed benefits include all of the benefit

---

[2] *Proceedings of the National Association of Insurance Commissioners*, I, (1977), p. 490.
[3] The Application of the Commissioners Annuity Reserve Method to Fixed Single Premium Deferred Annuities, *Transactions* XXXIV, p. 103.

streams guaranteed under the contract, including annuity benefits, death benefits, and nonforfeiture benefits. For each future guaranteed benefit, it is then
necessary to calculate the present value of that benefit, as of the date of
valuation, less the present value of future "valuation considerations" which are
required to be paid under the contract, with all present values taken at the
valuation basis of mortality and interest. The CARVM reserve is the greatest
of the net present values which have been so calculated. CARVM can thus be
considered a "worst case" valuation method, in that the reserve for a particular policy is calculated taking into account the scenario which maximizes
the liability.

There are several interesting points about these mechanics. First,
CARVM requires explicit recognition of future nonforfeiture values in the
future benefit component of the reserve calculation. This is unlike U.S. life
insurance reserve methodology, where only death benefits and endowment
payments are explicitly taken into account.[4] Second, in order to calculate the
CARVM reserve in the general case for a particular annuity policy, it is
necessary to determine every possible future death benefit, nonforfeiture value,
and annuity payment under the contract at the end of each contract year, and
then to calculate the present value of each of these benefits. As a typical
annuity policy may have at least half a dozen annuity options, and as there
may be dozens of anniversaries where annuitization is possible, it follows that
hundreds of present values theoretically would need to be determined in order
to calculate the CARVM reserve for a single policy. Luckily, with many
policy designs, it is possible to immediately determine which benefit will
produce the greatest present value, thus eliminating the need to calculate all
but a few future benefits. This will be examined in detail in the examples
which follow.

Actuaries sometimes confuse the accumulation rate of interest and the
valuation basis of interest and mortality under CARVM. To use CARVM,
two separate procedures are performed. In the first phase, it is necessary to
calculate future guaranteed benefits. This may involve accumulating the policy fund, and it may involve applying the fund at various times to purchase
annuity benefits using guaranteed annuity purchase rates. When accumulating
in this manner, guaranteed fund accumulations are used (including any
guarantees, such as excess interest, declared since issue), and when applying
the fund to determine annuity benefits, the guaranteed annuity purchase rates

---

[4] Although the NAIC recommends that nonforfeiture values be considered when
setting liabilities for life policies, and some states, such as California, have issued guidelines
requiring that such values be appropriately considered in setting reserve liabilities.

in the contract are utilized. The second phase of CARVM involves discounting the benefits derived in the first phase. The valuation rate of interest and, where appropriate, the valuation basis of mortality are used in this discounting. It is important to realize that the accumulation basis and the valuation basis are completely separate, but both are used in CARVM, regardless of their relationship.[5]

Consider the SPDA described below:

Single Premium: 10,000
No Front End Load
Guaranteed Interest: 10% in years 1 through 5
                             4% thereafter

Surrender Charge:	Policy Year	Percent of Fund
	1	7%
	2	6
	3	5
	4	4
	5	3
	6	2
	7	1
	8 and later	0

Valuation Interest Rate: 8%
Death Benefit Equal to Cash Surrender Value

Table 5.1, on the following page, shows the guaranteed fund accumulation value, as well as the cash surrender value, at the end of each of the first 10 policy durations.

Assuming that no excess interest is granted to the fund, Table 5.2, on the following page, shows the present value at 8% as of the issue date (policy year of valuation 0) and as of each of the first five policy anniversaries of each future cash surrender value.

---

[5] An exception occurs in the calculation of Federally Prescribed Tax Reserves, where the guaranteed interest rate used to determine the future benefits under the annuity cannot exceed the rate which is used for tax valuation purposes.

TABLE 5.1

Policy Year	Fund	Cash Value
0	10,000	9,300
1	11,000	10,230
2	12,100	11,374
3	13,310	12,645
4	14,641	14,055
5	16,105	15,622
6	16,749	16,414
7	17,419	17,245
8	18,116	18,116
9	18,841	18,841
10	19,594	19,594

TABLE 5.2

DEVELOPMENT OF CARVM RESERVES

Future Policy Year	Cash Value	Policy Anniversary of Valuation					
		0	1	2	3	4	5
0	9,300	9,300					
1	10,230	9,472	10,230				
2	11,374	9,751	10,531	11,374			
3	12,645	10,038	10,841	11,708	12,645		
4	14,055	10,331	11,157	12,050	13,014	14,055	
5	15,622	*10,632*	*11,483*	*12,401*	*13,393*	*14,465*	*15,622*
6	16,414	10,344	11,171	12,065	13,030	14,072	15,198
7	17,245	10,062	10,867	11,737	12,676	13,690	14,785
8	18,116	9,788	10,571	11,416	12,329	13,316	14,381
9	18,841	9,425	10,179	10,994	11,873	12,823	13,849
10	19,594	9,076	9,802	10,586	11,433	12,348	13,335

For each of the first 5 years, the cash value which produces the largest present value is shown in *bold-faced italic*. For example, as of the end of the second policy year, the present value of the second year-end cash value is 11,374, the present value of the third year-end cash value is 11,708, and the present value of the tenth year-end cash value is 10,586. Discounting is at interest only, ignoring mortality, as the surrender benefits and death benefits are equal. As can be seen, the cash surrender value at the end of the 5th year always produces the greatest present value for valuations on each of the first five policy years. Thus, the CARVM reserve at, for example, the second policy year-end would be 12,401, the present value of the fifth policy year value.

This example illustrates how it is often possible to determine in advance which duration will produce the largest present value. In general, for an SPDA the following considerations apply:

(1) If guaranteed annuity purchase rates are calculated on a less liberal basis than the valuation basis, and if the cash surrender value is used to determine the guaranteed annuity payments, then the future guaranteed annuity payments will never enter into the CARVM calculation, because the present value of the guaranteed annuity payments will always be less than the cash value at the date of annuitization.

(2) For a contract with no surrender charges, if the guaranteed fund accumulation rate is less than the valuation interest rate, then the cash value which will generate the largest present value is the cash value at the valuation date. If such a contract has a guaranteed accumulation rate which is greater than the valuation rate for a number of years after the valuation date, and thereafter is less than or equal to the valuation rate, then the cash value which will generate the largest present value is the cash value at the end of the last year for which the accumulation rate is in excess of the valuation rate. If such a contract has guaranteed accumulation rates which are always in excess of the valuation interest rate, then the cash value which will produce the largest present value is the cash value at the latest possible maturity date.

(3) For policies with surrender charges, if the combined effect of the guaranteed interest rate plus the reduction in the surrender charge exceeds the valuation rate for exactly n years, then the greatest present value will occur by discounting the cash value at the end of the nth contract year. If the combined effect of the guaranteed rate plus the reduction in the surrender charge is sometimes greater and other times less than the valuation interest rate in an alternating fashion, then it will be necessary to discount the cash

values at many points to find which has the greatest present value.[6]

In the above example, to see why it is true that the 6th year cash value has a lower present value than the 5th, we calculate the 5th and 6th year effective interest rates as

$$i_5 = \frac{CSV_5 - CSV_4}{CSV_4} = \frac{15,622 - 14,055}{14,055} = 11.15\%$$

and

$$i_6 = \frac{CSV_6 - CSV_5}{CSV_5} = \frac{16,414 - 15,622}{15,622} = 5.07\%.$$

Since the fifth year's (and all previous years') effective interest rate exceeds the valuation rate of 8%, and the sixth year's (and all subsequent years') effective interest rate is less than this rate, the fifth year cash value will produce the greatest present value for the first five years.[7] After the fifth year, the current cash value will produce the largest present value.

In many situations, it is often a simple matter to determine which cash value will produce the greatest present value using analytical methods. This is something which should be considered at the product design stage, as some product features make such analysis very difficult or impossible.

Mid-Policy Year Values and Continuous CARVM

A common question concerns the typical situation where the annuity contract has a surrender charge expressed as a percentage of the fund, where the percentage grades off at the beginning of each policy year. As an example, consider a contract with a 5% initial surrender charge which grades off 1% for each full policy year. Assume that the projected guaranteed fund balance at the end of the second policy year is 10,000, producing a cash surrender value of 9600. If one more day is projected, to the beginning of the third year, the cash value jumps to 9700 (plus whatever additional interest may have accrued

---

[6] Adapted from Jaffe.

[7] Note that the effective interest rate is approximately the guaranteed interest rate, plus the decrease in the surrender charge.

overnight). In this case, projecting to the beginning of each policy year would produce a larger present value than discounting to the end.

However, CARVM requires calculating present values based on benefits as of the end of each policy year. The language specifically states end of year values should be used, and examples found in the NAIC *Proceedings*[8] use end of year methodology, even though beginning of the year methodology would have produced larger reserves for the policies shown in these examples. Thus it is clear that drafters of CARVM intended for end of year values to be used, even though they realized (as evidenced by the example in the *Proceedings*) that typical SPDA designs would produce larger reserves if beginning of the year values had been used.

New York is the only state where a literal interpretation of CARVM is that reserves be calculated using the maximum present values of benefits on *any* day (i.e., not just end of year benefits). It should be noted that New York law does not define CARVM using the model language, which is quoted at the beginning of this chapter. Rather, New York law is silent on CARVM methodology, and states, "the Superintendent shall, by regulation, issue guidelines for the application of the reserve valuation method to annuity... contracts."[9] New York regulations then define CARVM as follows:

"(ii) The minimum reserve for contracts with unconditional surrender charges or with conditional surrender charges not considered to be meaningful shall be the greater of (1) the contract cash surrender value and (2) the greatest of the respective excesses of the present values, at the date of valuation, of the future cash surrender values provided for by the contract *on any day* of each respective contract year, over the present value, at the date of valuation, of any future valuation net considerations derived from future gross considerations, required by the terms of the contract that become payable prior to such day of such respective contract year."[10]

So, New York's requirement to use all cash values, rather than only end of year values, is consistent with New York law, which differs significantly from other states on this point.

Recently a number of other state insurance departments have expressed a preference for the continuous CARVM methodology used in New York.

---

[8] NAIC *Proceedings*, 1976 Volume II, pp. 637-638.
[9] *New York Insurance Law*, Section 4217(6)(D).
[10] *New York Regulations*, Section 95.11(C)(5)(ii). (Emphasis added)

Some state regulators prefer the continuous approach for all annuities, while others only prefer the technique for certain types of annuities, such as those where the policyholder can withdraw funds without incurring a surrender penalty for a limited window period after the policy anniversary. Actuarial Guideline XXXIII, which was intended to address several technical CARVM issues, has ambiguous wording relative to the continuous CARVM issue. According to one of the drafters of the Guideline, the language is intentionally ambigous on this point to allow for varying viewpoints. Unless otherwise specified, the remaining examples in this text use standard CARVM methodology as specified in the NAIC model.

COMMON PRODUCT FEATURES

In practice, a number of common product features can create complications in calculating the CARVM reserve for SPDA's. Some of these are discussed below.

Contingent Benefits

Two contingent benefits are common in SPDA's. These are benefits which are not elected by the annuitant but which are contingent upon the occurance of events specified in the contract.

Death Benefit in Excess of Cash Surrender Value

Many SPDA's have a death benefit prior to annuitization equal to the fund value before deduction of surrender charges. Additionally, some SPDA's allow for a minimum death benefit equal to the premium paid.

Actuarial Guideline XXXIII requires that each benefit be considered in calculation of the CARVM reserve.[11] In practice a separate death benefit reserve is often calculated and added to basic CARVM reserve. This death benefit reserve is calculated as the present value of the excess of the death

---

[11] When Guideline XXXIII was first adopted, some interpreted it as requiring separate calculations for each contingent benefit, with the contingent benefit creating additional reserves only if the separate reserve for that benefit exceeded the basic CARVM reserve. The NAIC's Life and Health Actuarial Task Force rejected this interpretation in late 1995.

benefit over the cash surrender value. One common approximation is to set the mortality reserve equal to the sum of the present values at valuation interest and mortality, of the cost of each of the future excesses of death benefit over cash surrender value.

A more exact approach is to calculate the mortality reserve as the sum of the present values at valuation interest and mortality of the cost of excess death benefits[12] only up to the end of the policy year corresponding to the cash value which accounts for the largest present value incorporated in the basic CARVM reserve. This is because if the policy value is paid in cash (the assumption underlying the basic reserve) the policy must be cash-surrendered, precluding the possibility of dying later.

Nursing Home Waiver

Some companies have begun offering a nursing home waiver, where the surrender charges are waived if the annuitant enters a nursing home. An additional reserve is calculated for this benefit in the same manner as the mortality reserve, with assumed rates of nursing home confinement applied to the future excesses of fund over cash value.

Bailout Provisions

A number of deferred annuities with surrender charges contain a provision that if the current, nonguaranteed fund accumulation interest rate falls more than a specified amount below the initial rate, then all or part of the surrender charge will be waived for a limited time period. These so called *bailout provisions* were designed to allay the fears of prospective purchasers who might otherwise feel that the insurance company would be tempted to lower the attractive original interest rate after their money had been locked into a contract with significant surrender charges.

Clearly, if the bailout provision is in effect at the date of valuation, so that the surrender charge is not then currently in effect, this "phantom" surrender charge should not be considered when calculating the contribution of the current cash value to the CARVM equation. As a practical matter, most of

---

[12] Technically the reserve should be the excess of the death benefit over the projected CARVM reserve, but the excess of the death benefit over the cash value is often used, as it is conservative and easier to calculate.

the time this will result in a CARVM reserve equal to the current fund value in such a situation. However, the appropriateness of taking future surrender charges into account when calculating CARVM reserves for contracts with bailout provisions is not at first clear if the bailout provision is inoperable at the time of the valuation.

In 1985 the NAIC adopted Actuarial Guideline XIII which states that the value of future guaranteed benefits under CARVM may not be reduced by significant contingent surrender charges[13] which may not be available upon cash surrender. This guideline clears up the situation with respect to bailout provisions by making most such future contingent surrender charges inappropriate for use in calculating CARVM reserves.

New York Regulation 126 requires that reserves for contracts with significant[14] contingent surrender charges be the greater of (a) the fund at date of valuation without deduction of any surrender charge, and (b) the standard CARVM reserve[15] calculated by ignoring surrender charges when determining future cash values.

The difference in these two requirements becomes apparent in the following annuity:

> Premium: 10,000
> Interest Guarantee: 8% for 2 years, 4% thereafter
> Surrender Charge: 5%/4/3/2/1/0
> Bailout Interest Rate: 7%
> Valuation Rate: 6%
> Long Life Rate: 5.5%

Projected funds and cash values at issue and at each of the first four policy year-ends are given in the Table 5.3, on the following page. Table 5.3 also shows the present values at issue at the valuation rate, of each year-end cash value, ignoring the bailout provision.

---

[13] Bailout surrender charges are significant if they take effect at interest rates greater than the maximum valuation rate permissible for life insurance of 20 years or more duration (the long life rate).

[14] New York uses the same definition of significant as the NAIC.

[15] As described earlier in this chapter, New York generally deviates from standard CARVM in requiring *beginning-of-year*, rather than *end-of-year*, values. However, for this (b) test used for bailout contracts, Regulation 126 uses standard CARVM with end-of-year values.

TABLE 5.3

Policy Year	Fund	Cash Value	Present Value
0	10,000	9,500	9,500
1	10,800	10,260	9,679
2	11,664	11,197	9,965
3	12,131	11,767	9,880
4	12,616	12,364	9,793

Under the NAIC guideline, we find that the bailout is significant (since the bailout rate exceeds the long life rate). However, only the surrender charges beginning at duration 3 are contingent.[16] Applying the NAIC rule (ignoring significant contingent surrender charges), we get the values shown in the following table. Under the NAIC Guideline, the CARVM reserve at issue is · 10,185.

TABLE 5.4

Policy Year	Cash Value	Cash Value Ignoring Contingent SC	Present Value
0	9,500	9,500	9,500
1	10,260	10,260	9,679
2	11,197	11,197	9,965
3	11,767	12,131	10,185
4	12,364	12,616	9,993

However, a literal interpretation of the New York Regulation requires that all surrender charges be ignored if contingent surrender charges exist. This results in the values shown in Table 5.5 on the following page, showing that the CARVM reserve in New York is 10,381.

---

[16] Surrender charges for durations 1 and 2 are not contingent as the interest rate is guaranteed to be 8%, and can never fall below the 7% bailout rate.

TABLE 5.5

Duration	Fund	Present Value
0	10,000	10,000
1	10,800	10,189
2	11,664	10,381
3	12,131	10,185
4	12,616	9,993

Market Value Adjustments

A number of SPDA's contain *market value adjustments* (MVA's), which attempt to adjust the cash surrender value to take into account movements in interest rates during the time since the premium was originally deposited with the company. Thus, if the annuity was originally purchased with interest rates at the 8% level and two years later interest rates had risen to 10%, the MVA would lower the cash value of the contract in order to account for the decrease in the value of the assets purchased by the company to back the annuity due to the increase in interest rates. MVA's are expressed in formula form rather than referring specifically to the assets underlying the annuity. Input to the formula may include the original interest rate credited, the rate credited at the time of surrender, and the rate credited on newly issued policies. Generally MVA's serve to decrease or increase the cash value, but some companies have MVA's which adjust in a downward direction only.

Questions asked include (1) whether an MVA should be recognized, if operable, when calculating the cash value at the date of valuation, and (2) to what extent possible future MVA's should be taken into account when calculating future cash values under CARVM.

In the absence of guidance to the contrary, assuming the underlying assets are held in the insurer's general account and not in a separate account,[17] MVA's should be excluded from all calculations under CARVM, both at the date of valuation and when calculating future cash values. This is because the assets underlying the CARVM liabilities are not revalued under statutory accounting principles, and it would be inconsistent to adjust the liabilities to take into account interest rate changes without also adjusting the assets.

The NAIC model Modified Guaranteed Annuity Regulation requires that the assets backing MVA annuities be held in a separate account. The NAIC

---

[17] A separate account is a group of segregated assets accounted for separately from the insurer's general account, and usually held at market value.

model gives broad guidance as to reserve requirements, with minimum reserves equal to the cash surrender value *including* the effect of the MVA. Very few states have adopted this NAIC model.

New York's Regulation 127 defines required treatment of MVA annuity contracts. New York allows the insurer to hold underlying assets either in a separate account or in the general account.

For New York contracts with underlying assets held in a separate account and valued at market, the reserve is the greater of (a) or (b), defined by

(a) the cash surrender value at the date of valuation, *including* the effect of the MVA, and

(b) the present value of the contract benefits that are guaranteed.

The present value in (b) is taken at one of the following rates (which must be consistently applied):

(1) The annual market yield of the underlying assets, reduced by
   (i) investment expenses,
   (ii) 2.5% for high-yield obligations (i.e., junk bonds), and
   (iii) 0.25% for adverse deviation.
(2) Moody's Corporate Bond Yield Average for the month preceding the valuation date.

For New York contracts with underlying assets held in the general account, or in a separate account, but held at book value, the reserve is the greater of (a) or (b), defined by

(a) the cash surrender value at the date of valuation, *excluding* the effect of the MVA, and

(b) the present value of the contract benefits that are guaranteed, such present value assuming a "B" type contract.[18,19]

To qualify for these liberalized minimum reserves, certain requirements must be met regarding the underlying assets, and the extent to which the assets and liabilities are "matched" (a topic discussed in Chapter 8).

---

[18] B type contracts are defined later in this chapter.
[19] Additionally, such contracts come under the cash flow testing requirements of Regulation 126.

For the general account product, the cash surrender value that is reflected in the reserve excludes the effect of the MVA because the assets underlying the liability are not revalued to market. Again, it would be inconsistent to adjust the value of the liabilities to take into account interest rate change without also adjusting the value of the assets, assuming a reasonable match between the assets and liabilities.

Free Partial Withdrawals

Many single premium deferred annuities with surrender charges contain *free partial withdrawals* (FPW's), where the policyholder has the right to withdraw a specified percentage[20] of the accumulation fund value annually without incurring the surrender charge. Often, this right is restricted to a period, such as 30 days, after each anniversary date.

Companies have handled FPW's in at least two ways. The aggregate approach adjusts the surrender charges to reflect FPW's. For example, if a contract allows 10% of the fund to be withdrawn on each anniversary, a company using the aggregate approach would reduce each surrender charge by 10%[21] in order to approximate the effect of the FPW's.

The other method of handling FPW's is the seriatim method. Here the company considers each and every partial withdrawal which could be made. Thus, it would project such a policy to the next anniversary both assuming no partial withdrawal is made and assuming a full partial withdrawal is made. It is easy to see that a giant "tree" is generated, and, depending upon policy design, it is not always possible to use grouping methods when calculating the liabilities in practice. This is the main reason that some companies have used the aggregate approach.

A number of state insurance departments have taken issue with the aggregate approach, and have required companies which use this approach to revalue their liabilities using the seriatim method. One of the arguments used by these departments is that, depending upon the policy design, it is often true that the aggregate method gives lower reserves than the seriatim method, which is generally considered to be closer to a more literal interpretation of CARVM principles.

---

[20] Some contracts allow all or part of the interest or excess interest to be withdrawn penalty-free, rather than specifying a percentage of the fund value.

[21] That is, a 5% surrender charge would be treated as a 4.5% charge.

Annuity Purchase Rates

In order to encourage annuitization, a number of companies provide incentives in the form of purchase rate enhancements. Three types of enhancements are common:

Purchase Rates More Favorable than Guarantees

In practice, companies generally use current annuity purchase rates which are more liberal than those guaranteed in the contract, since annuitants would otherwise withdraw their fund balances at time of annuitization and purchase immediate annuities on the open market. This practice can produce large discontinuities in the basic CARVM reserve at the annuitization date. Actuarial Guideline XXXIII deals with the situation where the contract **guarantees** that the company will offer, at the time of annuitization, the rates offered to new purchasers of immediate annuities. For such contracts, the basic CARVM reserve shall be no less than 93% of the contract's fund value at time of valuation.

Waiver of Surrender Charge

Companies commonly waive the surrender charge in the event of annuitization. Sometimes this benefit is limited to policies that have been in force a minimum number of years (such as 5 or 10) and/or that annuitize for a stated minimum number of annuity payments (i.e., only if a 10 year certain or longer annuity is chosen). In the basic CARVM calculation, when the annuity benefits are valued, the entire fund should of course be applied to the applicable guaranteed purchase rates. The use of conservative guaranteed purchase rates generally eliminates any effect this feature may have on CARVM reserves, although problems may occur if short term certain options, such as 5-years certain, are allowed. If the contract guarantees that current annuity purchase rates may be used at time of annuitization, then, as discussed above, the CARVM reserve is no less than 93% of the fund value at time of valuation.

Two Tiered Interest Credits

Some companies have developed contracts which effectively accumulate two separate funds: one which is used to determine nonforfeiture values and death benefits, and another which is used to calculate the amount applied toward annuitization and, possibly, the death benefit. Typically, the funds differ in that the second is credited interest at a rate which is a specified amount (such as 1%) higher than that used for the first fund.

To value these contracts, the first fund is used to determine the greatest present value of cash surrender values. Then the second fund is used to calculate fund balances which are applied to purchase annuities at guaranteed purchase rates. These annuity benefits are then discounted to the date of annuitization using the valuation rate of interest and mortality, and then discounted at interest only to the date of valuation. The CARVM reserve is the greatest present value produced by these two sets of calculations. CARVM calculations may be greatly complicated since the annuity benefits must be taken into account.

An important factor in whether the second fund generates benefits which become significant in the CARVM calculation is how the guaranteed annuity purchase rates compare to the valuation basis of mortality and interest. If guaranteed purchase rates are high rates, such as those based on the valuation rates, the second fund will contribute significant benefits. However, if the guaranteed purchase rates are very low compared to the valuation basis, this may not be the case.

It should be noted that two tiered contracts often guarantee the right to use current annuity purchase rates at time of annuitization. If this is the case, the Actuarial Guideline XXXIII requirement that the CARVM reserve be at least equal to 93% of the fund value at time of valuation comes into effect, with the 93% applied to the fund used to purchase annuity benefits.

Actuarial Guideline XXXIII does not address the case where the company allows the use of current annuity purchase rates at time of annuitization, but where this practice is not guaranteed by the contract. Note that in this case there can be discontinuities in the reserve before and after annuitization, particularly for two-tiered annuities. As with all reserves, it is necessary for the valuation actuary to be satisfied that the reserves make good and sufficient provision for the future obligations of the company. In some circumstances additional reserves should be established beyond those required by

Interest Index

Some SPDA's guarantee to credit a minimum rate such as 4%, but also guarantee that the rate credited will not be less than a specified index.[22] The

---

[22] For example, 110% of the 90-day Treasury bill rate, less 0.50%.

NAIC Interest-Indexed Annuity Contracts Model Regulation addresses such products, and provides as follows:

> "In the calculation of reserves for interest-indexed annuity contracts, future guarantees will be determined by assuming that future interest crediting rates will be equal to the statutory valuation interest rate for such contracts as defined in the Standard Valuation Law."[23]

This means that the CARVM reserve is not increased to recognize that the index interest rate might be higher than the valuation interest rate. It also eliminates the possibility of decreasing the CARVM reserve to reflect a guaranteed rate less than the valuation rate. Thus, the greatest present value will occur by discounting the cash value at the end of the contract year with the lowest surrender charge. If there is a contract year with no surrender charge (or other difference between the fund balance and the cash surrender value), the CARVM reserve will equal the fund balance on the valuation date.

Since the NAIC model has not been adopted by any state, most companies ignore such interest-index features unless in effect at the time of valuation, except to the extent that cash flow testing[24] indicates a need for additional reserves. Of course, it is the actuary's responsibility to ensure the sufficiency of reserves, and an index with a high probability of "kicking in" should be accounted for in some explicit manner when projecting future benefits.

PRACTICAL CONSIDERATIONS IN THE CALCULATION OF CARVM RESERVES

A number of practical considerations in the calculation of CARVM reserves are discussed on the following page.

---

[23] The NAIC model also provides for a Statement of Actuarial Opinion for Interest-Indexed Annuity Contracts with the minimum reserve increased to 115% of the reserve otherwise required if the statement is not filed. The requirement of a special Statement of Actuarial Opinion for Interest-Indexed Annuity Contracts would not be in effect until a state actually formally adopts the model.

[24] Cash flow testing is discussed in Chapter 8.

Calendar Year Valuations

In most of the examples so far, we have assumed that the valuation was performed on a policy anniversary date. Generally, of course, this is not the case. When calculating CARVM reserves on an off-anniversary date, the same principles apply as above. When calculating future guaranteed bene-fits, the fund balance as of the valuation date is the valuation date is accumulated using future guaranteed rates of interest. Many companies guarantee current interest rates on a policy year basis. In such a case, current rates which are guaranteed for remaining fractional policy years are taken into account.[25] Also, as before, the fund balance is accumulated to the end of each future policy year in order to determine benefits as of the end of each policy year. A common mistake is to calculate the benefits at the end of future calendar years rather than policy years.

Note that there are other methods of calculating calendar year CARVM reserves. For example, several companies calculate the CARVM reserve as of the next policy year end, and then discount it to the date of valuation.

Current Cash Values

Although CARVM does not technically utilize the current cash value if the date of valuation is on an off anniversary date, Exhibit 8, Paragraph G of the NAIC Blank requires that the total reserve for each policy be not less than the corresponding cash value.[26] Because of this requirement, the current cash value should be substituted for the CARVM reserve for a policy, if greater. Note that the cash value is compared to the entire CARVM reserve, including any applicable death benefit reserve.

Grouping Methods

It is traditional and generally accepted actuarial practice to calculate reserves using a group approach rather than on a seriatim basis, and to assume that issues for the group of policies occur in the middle of the issue year, except that in cases where significant skewing is known to occur it is common practice to adjust the average issue date to take this skewing into account.

---

[25] In the calculation of Federally Prescribed Tax Reserves, the lower of the actual guaranteed interest rate and the valuation rate is used to accumulate the fund.

[26] See discussion in Chapter 7.

The Standard Valuation Law allows "group methods and approximate averages for fractions of a year or otherwise." In particular, a group approach may be acceptable for single premium deferred annuities, where policies with the same guaranteed accumulation rate and issue year are grouped, and where the average issue date is assumed to be the middle of the period for which such guaranteed rate was available (adjusted for significant skewing). However, acceptability of the group approach may be hampered by the inclusion of some complicating policy design features, such as "two-tiered" interest guarantees.

Change-in-Fund Valuation Basis

The Standard Valuation Law allows the use of either an *issue year basis* or a *change-in-fund basis* for calculating the present values of future benefits under CARVM.[27] While these are technically not differences in CARVM, they affect the calculation of reserves under CARVM. Furthermore, different interest rates are appropriate depending upon which basis is used.

Under an issue year basis, the valuation interest rate is determined as of the issue date of the policy, and this rate is used for discounting all of the guaranteed future benefits under the policy ad remains constant throughout the life of the contract.[28] To this point, we have been tacitly assuming that an issue year basis is being employed.

Under a change-in-fund basis, the future benefits are discounted using different interest rates depending upon when the increase in the fund occurred which generated the specific benefits.[29]

The advantage to the company of using a change-in-fund basis is that the initial maximum valuation rate is usually greater than when an issue year method is used; however, if interest rates were to fall subsequent to the issue date, it is possible that the maximum rates applicable to increases in the fund could be less than if an issue year method had been used.

Change-in-fund basis valuation methodology is not defined precisely under CARVM, and different companies compute the reserves under this

---

[27] The change-in-fund basis may only be used if the contract has cash settlement options.

[28] Prior to annuitization in the case of a deferred annuity.

[29] Exhibit 1 to Appendix A of the NAIC's *Financial Condition Examiners Handbook* states, The change-in-fund basis values the original amount deposited at the interest rate in effect when it was deposited; all changes to the fund thereafter, including interest on the original deposit, are valued at the rates in effect when they occurred.

method using different methodologies. One reasonable method is to calculate CARVM reserves in the calendar year of issue using the change-in-fund valuation interest rate appropriate for that calendar year. In the next calendar year, CARVM reserves would be calculated using the valuation interest rate for the calendar year of issue to discount benefits attributable to all fund balances up to those in effect at the end of the first calendar year, and using the change-in-fund basis valuation interest rate for the second calendar year for any benefits attributable to funds in excess of this amount. Similarly, in subsequent years, any benefits due to the increase in the fund value would be valued using the then appropriate change-in-fund valuation rates. Net decreases in the aggregate balances would be treated on a Last-In-First-Out (LIFO) basis.[30] Note that the benefits are discounted separately. Thus, when calculating the second year reserve, the first year fund may produce a maximum present value when projected to the third year, and the second year change in fund may produce a maximum present value when projected to the seventh year. In such a case, these two present values of benefits in different years are added together to arrive at the CARVM reserve.[31]

For example, consider an SPDA with no front-end load with a 5% surrender charge grading down 1% each year and reaching zero in the 6th year. Guaranteed interest rates are 10% for years one through three, 8.5% for years four to six, and 4% thereafter. No current interest is applied in excess of the guaranteed rate. Assume that the appropriate change-in-fund maximum valuation rate is 10% in 1990 and 9% in 1991.[32]

For a 10,000 policy issued July 1, 1990, we have the values shown in the following table.

TABLE 5.6

Date	Fund	Surrender Value
7/01/90	10,000	9,500
12/31/90	10,488	9,964
12/31/91	11,537	11,076

---

[30] That is, decreases are netted against the portion attributable to the most recent calendar year.

[31] Another reasonable method involves determining the change in fund from the aggregate fund balance for a group of policies.

[32] These are not actual rates, and are used for illustration purposes only.

As of 12/31/90, the fund consists of one portion, all 1990 money. The largest present value of future guaranteed benefits is the present value of the cash value on the third policy anniversary,[33] which is

$$(10,488)\left(\frac{(1.10)^{2.5}}{(1.10)^{2.5}}\right)(.97) = 10,173$$

which is therefore the CARVM reserve at the end of 1990.

As of 12/31/91, the fund consists of two parts: a 1990 part of 10,488 and a 1991 part equal to $11,537 - 10,488 = 1,049$.

For the 1990 part, the largest present value of future guaranteed benefits is again the present value of the cash value on the third policy anniversary,

$$(10,488)\left(\frac{(1.10)^{1.5}}{(1.10)^{1.5}}\right)(.97) = 10,173.$$

For the 1991 part, the largest present value of future guaranteed benefits is the present value of the cash value on the sixth policy anniversary,[34]

$$(1049)\left(\frac{(1.10)^{1.5}(1.085)^{3}}{(1.09)^{4.5}}\right)(1.00) = 1,049.$$

Therefore the CARVM reserve is $10,173 + 1,049 = 11,222$ at the end of 1991.

Actuarial Guideline XXXIII requires that the election of issue year or change in fund basis must be made at the issuance of the contract and must not change during the term of the contract without the prior written approval of the insurance commissioner.

---

[33] The present value of the cash value on the second policy anniversary is 96/97 of this amount as the valuation rate and guaranteed accumulation rate are equal for the first two years. The value of the fourth anniversary cash value is less because $98/97 < 1.10/1.085$.

[34] Since the annual drop in surrender charges more than offsets the effect of accumulating at 8.5% and discounting at 9%.

ANNUAL PREMIUM ANNUITIES
UNDER CARVM

The preceding principles also apply to annual premium annuities. The only difference is that the present value of appropriate future "valuation considerations" is subtracted from the present value of each of the future benefits, and these differences are compared to determine the CARVM reserve. Valuation considerations are defined to be the "portions of the respective gross considerations applied" under the contract.

As an example, consider the following annuity:

Annual Premium:	1,000
Front-End Load:	5% of premium, plus 25
Guaranteed Interest:	10% in years 1 through 5, 4% thereafter

Surrender Charge:	Policy Year	Percent of Fund
	1-5	5%
	6	4
	7	3
	8	2
	9	1
	10 and later	0

Valuation Interest Rate: 8.75%

Death Benefit equal to Cash Surrender Value

Table 5.7, on the following page, shows the guaranteed fund accumulation value, as well as the cash surrender value, at the end of each of the first 10 policy durations, just prior to payment of the next year's premium.

For each contract year of valuation, Table 5.8 on page 90 shows the present value of each of the first ten terminal cash values, the present value of future valuation considerations, and the difference. For each contract year of valuation, the greatest of these differences is shown in bold-faced italics.

TABLE 5.7

Policy Year	Fund	Cash Value
1	1,018	967
2	2,137	2,030
3	3,368	3,200
4	4,722	4,486
5	6,212	5,901
6	7,422	7,126
7	8,681	8,421
8	9,991	9,791
9	11,352	11,239
10	12,768	12,768

For example, as of the second contract year-end, the present value of the fifth year-end cash value is

$$\frac{5,901}{(1.0875)^3} = 4,588.$$

The present value of future valuation considerations, net of front-end load, is

$$[(.950)(1,000) - 25] \cdot \ddot{a}_{\overline{3}|} = 2,558.$$

The difference is

$$4,588 - 2,558 = 2,031.$$

Determination of CARVM reserves by analytical method is much more difficult for annual premium annuities than for SPDA's. It is not possible to calculate a simple effective interest rate for an annual premium product with a surrender charge, as the entire net premium enters into the present value of future valuation considerations, but not necessarily into the present value of future benefits, due to the effect of the surrender charge. Thus, as in the above example, the greatest of the present values can vary by contract year of valuation and is not easy to predict in advance.

TABLE 5.8

First value shown is the present value of the terminal cash value, second value shown is the present value of future valuation considerations, and the third value is the difference.

Future Policy Year	Cash Value	Policy Anniversary of Valuation					
		0	1	2	3	4	5
1	967	889	967				
		925	0				
		(36)	*967*				
2	2,030	1,716	1,867	2,030			
		1,776	925	0			
		(59)	942	2,030			
3	3,200	2,488	2,705	2,942	3,200		
		2,558	1,776	925	0		
		(70)	930	2,017	3,200		
4	4,486	3,207	3,488	3,793	4,125	4,486	
		3,277	2,558	1,776	925	0	
		(70)	930	2,018	3,200	4,486	
5	5,901	3,880	4,219	4,588	4,990	5,427	5,901
		3,938	3,277	2,558	1,776	925	0
		(59)	942	*2,031*	*3,214*	*4,502*	*5,901*
6	7,126	4,308	4,685	5,094	5,540	6,025	6,552
		4,546	3,938	3,277	2,558	1,776	925
		(239)	746	1,818	2,983	4,249	5,627
7	8,421	4,681	5,091	5,536	6,021	6,547	7,120
		5,106	4,546	3,938	3,277	2,558	1,776
		(424)	544	1,598	2,744	3,990	5,345
8	9,791	5,005	5,443	5,919	6,437	7,000	7,613
		5,620	5,106	4,546	3,938	3,277	2,558
		(615)	337	1,373	2,499	3,723	5,055
9	11,239	5,283	5,745	6,248	6,794	7,389	8,035
		6,093	5,620	5,106	4,546	3,938	3,277
		(810)	125	1,142	2,248	3,450	4,758
10	12,768	5,519	6,002	6,527	7,098	7,719	8,394
		6,527	6,093	5,620	5,106	4,546	3,938
		(1,009)	(91)	907	1,992	3,173	4,456

For each of the first 5 years, the cash value which produces the largest present value is shown in *bold-faced italics.*

FLEXIBLE PREMIUM ANNUITIES UNDER CARVM

CARVM requires that future valuation considerations "required by the terms of such contract" be taken into account. Because Flexible Premium Annuities do not generally require future premium payments, they are usually reserved as SPDAs, assuming at the time of valuation that no future premiums are paid. Indeed, an example in the NAIC *Proceedings*[35] takes this approach.

In a given situation, this produces reserves for Flexible Premium contracts which can either be greater than (in the case of a heavily back-end loaded product with temporary interest guarantees in excess of the valuation rate) or less than (in the case of a non-backloaded product with similar interest guarantees) corresponding reserves for a fixed premium product. For example, if the contract illustrated in Table 5.8 were a flexible premium product, the reserve on the first anniversary would be 1,012 instead of 967.

Once again, the valuation actuary should use judgment rather than mechanically applying CARVM. It may be more appropriate to hold fixed premium type reserves in some cases, particularly if the product were sold in such a manner that regular premiums are expected to be paid.

IMMEDIATE ANNUITIES

Immediate annuities (and life income currently payable under deferred annuity contracts) generally present no particular problems under CARVM. In the case of immediate annuities without cash surrender values, the CARVM reserve is equal to the present value of the annuity benefits, which is the same as the method prior to the adoption of CARVM. If an immediate annuity has cash surrender values, it is possible that the present value of one of these could exceed the present value of the annuity benefits.

Since the valuation interest rate allowed for immediate annuities is generally greater than that allowed for deferred annuities, the NAIC adopted Actuarial Guidelines IX and IXB, which define an immediate annuity as one where

    (a) the first payment is due not more than thirteen months from the annuity issue date,

---

[35] *Proceedings of the National Association of Insurance Commissioners*, I (1977), p. 545.

(b) succeeding payments are due at least annually for at least 5 years, and

(c) the underlying pattern of payments due in any contract year are not greater than 115% of those in the prior contract year.

In the case of a deferred annuity which annuitizes, or a settlement option arising from a life insurance policy or an annuity contract, most companies value the "new" immediate annuity at the valuation rate in effect at the date of annuitization. Guideline IX-B allows this practice, as well as the practice of using the rate in effect at the original issue date, but requires consistency from year to year in the method used.

Many immediate annuities provide that a specified number of payments will be made regardless of the survival of the annuitant. Often the payments during this certain period are separately valued as an annuity certain, with the remaining payments valued as a deferred annuity. For example, the reserve for a 5-year certain and life annuity is calculated as $\ddot{a}_{\overline{5}|} + {}_{5|}\ddot{a}_x$.

Note, however, that the interest rate used in calculating both parts is the rate appropriate for an immediate annuity, as the contract in its entirety qualifies as an immediate annuity.

Structured settlements are immediate annuities with "customized" payment patterns, which may include lump-sum payments. Structured settlements are often issued in conjunction with personal injury settlements, and so may be priced assuming substandard mortality. Guidelines IX-A and IX-B address special valuation considerations involving structured settlements, including the use of substandard mortality, and acceptable methods for valuing lump sum and increasing payments.

DETERMINATION OF APPROPRIATE INTEREST RATES UNDER THE STANDARD VALUATION LAW

The 1980 amendments to the Standard Valuation Law introduced a multitude of annuity valuation interest rate categories. The major categories are as follows:

(A) Single premium immediate annuities, and annuity benefits involving life contingencies arising from other annuities with cash settlement options and from guaranteed interest contracts with cash settlement options.

(B) Other annuities. This category is further broken down as follows:
   (1) Whether or not the policy offers cash settlement options. In this context, this means whether or not the policy has a provision for the withdrawal of cash.
   (2) Whether an issue year or a change in fund basis is to be used in the valuation. Note that only policies with cash settlement options are permitted to utilize a change in fund basis.
   (3) Whether or not the policy contains future interest guarantees applicable to considerations received more than one year from the issue date, or one year from the valuation date in the case of a change in fund basis.[36]
   (4) For annuities with cash settlement options, the number of years that interest rate guarantees are in excess of the long life rate.[37] This is referred to as the *guarantee duration.* For annuities with no cash settlement options, the guarantee duration is the number of years from the date of issue or date of purchase to the date annuity benefits are scheduled to commence.
   (5) The "plan type," where plan type is determined by the withdrawal rights as follows:
   Plan Type A – At any time the policyholder may withdraw funds only (1) with the adjustment to reflect changes in interest rates or asset values since receipt of the funds by the insurance company or (2) without such adjustment but in installments over a period of five years or more, or (3) as an immediate life annuity, or (4) no withdrawal permitted.
   Plan Type B – Before expiration of the interest rate guarantee, the policyholder may withdraw funds only (1) with adjustment to reflect changes in interest rates or asset values since receipt of the funds by the insurance company, or (2) without such adjustment but in installments over a period of five years or more, or (3) no withdrawal permitted. At the end of interest rate guarantee, funds may be withdrawn without such adjustment in single sum or installments over less than five years.

---

[36] Disagreement exists as to whether the intent is to include all future interest guarantees applicable to future premiums, or only to include guarantees which are in excess of the long life rate.
[37] The long life rate is the maximum valuation rate permissible for life insurance policies of more than 20 years duration.

Plan Type C – The policyholder may withdraw funds before expiration of interest rate guarantee in a single sum or installments over less than five years either (1) without adjustment to reflect changes in interest rates or asset values since receipt of the funds by the insurance company, or (2) subject only to a fixed surrender charge stipulated in the contract as a percentage of the fund.

Actuarial Guideline XXXIII specifies that different benefits under an SPDA may be valued assuming different plan types. In particular, when calculating the greatest present value of the cash values available under the contract, these benefit streams should generally be valued using interest rates applicable under Plan Type C. On the other hand, when valuing the greatest present value of the annuitization benefits available under the contract, Plan Type A interest rates are generally used, since the underlying assumption is that no cash surrender values will be exercised if the annuity benefits are elected. In this latter case, Guideline XXXIII defines the guarantee duration as the number of years from the original issue date of the contract to the date annuitization commences. This implies that different guarantee durations, and thus different valuation interest rates, are used in valuing the annuitization benefits that may be elected at different dates.

The maximum valuation rate permitted for the matrix of different possible combinations of plan characteristics outlined above is defined in the Standard Valuation Law as a function of 12 and 36 month trailing averages of the Moody's Corporate Bond Yield Average. As an indication of the complexity of this system, and to give an idea as to the various levels of interest rates allowed under these formulas, Appendix B shows the maximum valuation rates for calendar years 1981 through 1995.

EXERCISES

1. Consider the following SPDA:
   Guaranteed Interest:

Policy Year	Rate
1-3	10%
4-5	6
6+	4

   Surrender Charge:

Policy Year	Percent of Fund
1	7%
2	6
3	5
4	4
5	3
6	2
7	1
8+	0

   Assume the annuity fund value is $10,000 at the end of the 2nd policy year. Assume the long life rate is 5.5% and the current interest rate is 10%.

   (a) What is the CARVM reserve at duration 2 if the valuation rate is 7%. (Don't calculate, just write out the formula.)
   (b) What if the valuation rate is 5.5%?
   (c) What if the valuation rate is 7% and the contract has a bailout provision that the entire surrender charge is inoperable if the current rate were to fall below 8%?
   (d) How would part (a) change if the contract were issued in New York?

2. Consider the following annuity:
   Guaranteed Interest: 10% in years 1-3, 4% thereafter
   Surrender Charge: 6/5/4/3/2/1/0%
   Bailout Rate: 8%
   Premium: $10,000
   No loads or administrative fees
   Valuation Rate: 7%
   Long Life Rate: 5%

   (a) What is the CARVM reserve at issue under the NAIC model?
   (b) What is it under the New York guidelines?
   (c) How would each answer vary if the bailout rate were 6%?

3. Consider the following annuity with a market value adjustment:

	Cash Value
Before MVA	$10,000
After MVA	12,000

Assume the surrender charge is zero, and the present value of contract benefits is always less than the cash value.

(a) What is the CARVM reserve according to the NAIC regulation?
(b) What is the CARVM reserve assuming assets are held in the insurer's general account in a state other than New York which has not passed the NAIC model?
(c) What is the CARVM reserve in New York, assuming assets are held in the general account?
(d) What is the CARVM reserve in New York, assuming assets are held in the separate account?

4. Consider an SPDA issued 7/1/92 for a premium of $10,000 with no front-end load and a 5/4/3/2/1/0% surrender charge. Guaranteed rates are 9% for 4 years, and 4% thereafter. Assuming a change in fund valuation method, and appropriate valuation rates of 7% in 1992 and 4.5% in 1993, state the reserve on each of the following dates.

(a) 12/31/92   (b) 12/31/93

5. Consider the following annuity:

Premium: $1,000 per year
Front-end Load: 3%
Guaranteed Interest: 8% in years 1-3, 4% thereafter
Surrender Charge: 5/4/3/2/1/0%
Valuation Rate: 7%

(a) What is the CARVM reserve at the end of policy year 1, assuming the contract is an annual premium annuity?
(b) What if it were a flexible premium annuity, the $1,000 premium was paid in full at issue, and the second premium was not yet received at the end of policy year 1?

CHAPTER SIX

VALUATION OF VARIABLE PRODUCTS

Variable life insurance and annuity products are policies whose cash values are matched by assets held in a separate account[1] of the life insurance company. With variable products the policyholders bear the investment risk: the insurance company makes no guarantees as to investment performance.[2]

Problems arise in applying traditional reserve methodology to variable contracts. Both CRVM and CARVM define minimum reserves prospectively, based on future policy guarantees. However, variable products do not have future investment guarantees.

The NAIC's 1983 Variable Life Insurance Model Regulation states as follows:

"Reserve liabilities for variable life insurance policies shall be established under the Standard Valuation Law in accordance with actuarial procedures that recognize the variable nature of the benefits provided and any mortality guarantees."[3]

Similar language for annuity products is contained in the NAIC Variable Annuity Model Regulation.

---

[1] The separate account is a special segregation of assets underlying variable contracts. Other assets are held in the general account of the insurer.

[2] Except for any guaranteed minimum death benefits.

[3] The Model also defines additional reserve liabilities for the guaranteed minimum death benefit (GMDB) risk. These are discussed later in this chapter.

Actuaries are currently grappling with how to interpret the phrase "in accordance with actuarial procedures that recognize the variable nature of the product." As discussed below, some products, particularly front-end loaded contracts, easily lend themselves to reasonable interpretations of traditional reserve methodology. Other contracts, particularly those with back-end loads, are subject to multiple interpretations.

Note that some variable products offer a general account option. Reserve methodology for funds under this option is similar to that for non-variable contracts.

The remainder of this chapter looks at specific situations, including some where there is disagreement as to the proper reserve. Generally, reserve methodology for variable products is dependent upon product type, so the following discussion considers the major categories of products separately.

The following discussion focuses on three major product categories: annual premium variable life, single premium variable life, and variable annuities. Within the annual premium variable life category there are three sub-categories: flexible premium, fixed premium, and the hybrid product, which is combination of fixed and flexible.

FLEXIBLE PREMIUM AND HYBRID VARIABLE LIFE

A number of U.S. companies offer flexible premium variable life, also known as *variable universal life* (VUL). These products are similar to traditional universal life products in that mortality charges, calculated periodically and based on the actual net amount at risk, are deducted from an accumulation fund.

Expense charges may be either front-end charges deducted from the fund; rear-end charges, so that the policy cash value equals the fund less a predefined surrender charge; or a combination. Unlike fixed premium variable products, the death benefit does not necessarily vary with the investment performance of the separate account. The only significant difference between VUL products and traditional universal life is that the accumulation fund of the VUL policy is invested in and varies with the performance of the separate account, and the policyholders therefore bear the investment risk of the policy.

Hybrid products operate similarly to, and are reserved the same as, flexible premium products. Instead of a totally flexible premium, a scheduled premium concept is used, but the policyholder can pay additional premiums or skip premiums under a vanish provision.

VUL and hybrid products have recently become quite popular, and now account for virtually all variable life sales in the United States.

The Universal Life Model Regulation specifically exempts variable products. At any rate, application of the UL Model's reserve definition to VUL without modification would be inappropriate, as the UL Model uses a prospective technique based on a projection of future guaranteed benefits. In the absence of industry standards, it is the responsibility of the valuation actuary to ensure that the method used is appropriate for the particular product being valued.

For fully front-end loaded VUL products, it is generally felt that the policy's cash value represents a sufficient reserve in the absence of future mortality guarantees more liberal than the valuation basis. In the case where the first year load exceeds renewal loads by more than the first year CVRM expense allowance, the appropriateness of the cash value (net of surrender charges) as a reserve may be subject to question.

For back-end loaded products, the reserve held is typically a UL Model Regulation-type reserve, with one of the following interest rates used to project future benefits:

(1) For contracts with a fixed-account option, the long-term guaranteed rate in the fixed account.

(2) The valuation rate, less some or all of the contractual asset-based charges.[4]

(3) 4% interest.[5]

(4) The rate credited to policy loans.

Both the SEC and the Variable Life Model Regulation require that assets in the separate account be at least equal to the account value. However, statutory reserves for a back-end loaded variable product may be somewhat less than the account value, reflecting the presence of these surrender charges.

---

[4] That is, the charges which are assessed as a reduction to the investment earnings, including the the mortality and expense risk charge, and any other asset charges.

[5] The rate specified in tax law to be used in calculating guideline level premiums under the guideline premium test, as well as net single premiums under the cash value accumulation test.

As a result, surplus in the separate account is at least equal to the sum of all VUL expense allowance credits taken.[6] Otherwise the insurer would be at risk for any increase in underlying account values in the event that asset values improve.

For example, suppose a VUL contract has an account value of 10,000 and a surrender charge of 1,000. Suppose further that the insurer justifies holding a 9,000 reserve (equal to the cash value) using one of the methods described above. If the surrender charge reduces to zero next year, the insurer is scheduled to fund this amortization of the 1,000 surrender charge.

Should the underlying unit asset values double over the next year, the insurer would instead be forced to amortize 2,000, as the 1,000 excess of the account value over the reserve will have doubled. However, if the 1,000 excess of account value over reserve had been in the separate account, it too would have doubled, and the insurer would have additional funds available to pay for the increased amortization.

For both front-end and back-end loaded products, additional reserves are required in the event the product has a GMDB.

FIXED PREMIUM VARIABLE LIFE

One category of variable life features required periodic premiums which are fixed by the insurer. Typically, fixed premium variable life products are front-end loaded.[7] The death benefit is adjusted to reflect investment performance in one of two ways, referred to as the New York Life design and the Equitable design.

New York Life Design

Under the *New York Life design* the death benefit at any point in time is the original face amount times the ratio of the actual cash value to a hypothetical tabular cash value which has been calculated using an assumed interest rate

---

[6] Technically, most companies get the surplus in their general account, through a transfer. In this discussion, surplus means the excess of separate account assets over separate account liabilities.

[7] That is, explicit noncontingent charges are deducted for expenses. Back-end loaded products feature expense charges which are only charged to policyholders who lapse within a specified time period.

(AIR). Additionally, the policy has a guaranteed minimum death benefit (GMDB) equal to the initial face amount.

Ignoring the GMDB, reserves per 1,000 of current death benefit under the New York Life design are identical to those of a non-variable policy with the same current death benefit, issue age, and duration. Additional reserves, discussed later in this section, must be held for the GMDB risk.

Equitable Design

Under the *Equitable Design*, any net investment earnings over AIR are used to purchase variable paid up additions at net single premium rates using AIR; if net investment earnings are less than AIR, paid-up additions are canceled (effectively "negative" paid-up additions are purchased). A GMDB is provided in that if the paid-up additions are negative in total, this negative amount is carried forward notionally (and is used to offset future positive paid-up additions), but it does not affect the actual death benefit currently paid.

Reserves for the basic policy under the Equitable design are equal to tabular reserves calculated for a nonvariable policy of the same face amount, issue age, and duration. Reserves for the paid-up additions (if positive) are equal to those for similar nonvariable paid-up additions. Additional reserves must be held for the GMDB risk.

Thus, for both fixed premium variable life designs, reserves are based on traditional methodology and can be calculated using standard factor per 1,000 techniques. In both cases, additional reserves must be held for the GMDB risk. These are discussed later in this section.

True fixed premium variable life products represent a dwindling portion of the variable life market. The majority of new business is written through flexible premium or hybrid products.

Both the Equitable design and the New York Life design are illustrated in Figure 6.1, on the following page, where the shaded area represents the tabular cash values. These are traditional cash values calculated with interest equal to the AIR. If the guaranteed death benefit is G, the actual cash value at time t is Z, and the tabular cash value is Y, then the current death benefit for the contract, ignoring the GMDB, is

(1) $G \times Z/Y$ for a New York Life design product, and

(2) $G + (Z-Y)/A_{x+t}$ for an Equitable design product, where A_{x+t} is calculated at the AIR.

FIGURE 6.1

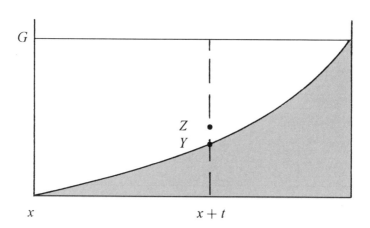

SINGLE PREMIUM VARIABLE LIFE

There are two basic types of "single premium" variable life.

Flexible Single Premium

Flexible single premium variable life is marketed as a single premium product. However, the contract gives the policyholder the right to make future premium payments, and typically is identical mechanically to a VUL contract. Reserve considerations are exactly the same as for VUL contracts. If a GMDB is provided, appropriate reserves must be held.

Fixed Single Premium

Fixed single premium variable life does not allow payment of premiums after the initial single premium. These contracts generally provide GMDB's, with gross premiums calculated based on an AIR. Fixed single premium contracts may be of the Equitable method, the New York Life method, or may use Universal Life-type mechanics to generate cash values. Reserve considerations are identical to regular premium contracts of the same type.

Since the introduction of tax law changes in 1988, the popularity of both types of single premium variable life has declined substantially.

VARIABLE ANNUITIES

As with the application of CRVM to variable life insurance, problems exist in applying CARVM to variable annuities, as CARVM is a prospective reserve method which considers discounted values of future policy guarantees.

For front-end loaded variable annuities, it is generally felt that the cash value is a good and sufficient reserve. However, as with VUL, there is debate over how to properly treat back-end loaded products. Some of the same methods proposed for VUL have also been suggested as alternatives for determining an appropriate interest rate to use in a CARVM-type variable annuity approach. Note that surplus in the separate account should at least equal the excess of account value over reserves.

Additional reserves should be carried for any death benefit guaranteed other than the cash surrender value. Such guarantees include return of premium provisions.

GUARANTEED MINIMUM DEATH BENEFITS (GMDB) RESERVES: FLEXIBLE PREMIUM LIFE PRODUCTS

Many variable life insuance products contain a guaranteed minimum death benefit (GMDB). The NAIC's Variable Life Insurance Model Regulation requires that an additional reserve be established for policies which contain GMDB's. This reserve is required to be carried in the general account of the insurer. The Model Regulation specifies different calculations for fixed and flexible premium variable life contracts.

The typical flexible premium variable life contract has a GMDB only for the grace period during which the funds under the contract are insufficient to support the deductions necessary to maintain the coverage in force. The GMDB reserve for a flexible premium variable contract is defined in the NAIC Variable Life Insurance Model Regulation as the term cost of the GMDB provided under the contract assuming an immediate one-third depreciation in the current value of the separate account assets, followed by a net investment return equal to the valuation interest rate. Note that the term reserves are based on the guarantees under the contract and are not limited to one year.

Example: Flexible Premium VUL Design

Consider a VUL policy which during the first five years has a $200,000 GMDB, provided that minimum cumulative premiums are paid.

At the end of year three, the policyholder has paid premiums equal to five years' minimum cumulative premiums. Thus, regardless of whether additional premiums are paid, there is a GMDB of $200,000 for the next two years.

The GMDB reserve would be the cost of the term insurance provided assuming an immediate 1/3 drop in the value of the assets underlying the separate account. One interpretation is to hold the excess of a traditional $200,000 two year net single premium over the reserve that the company would hold for the policy under the assumption of an immediate 1/3 drop in the asset value of the separate account and future investment performance equal to the valuation rate.

GMDB RESERVES:
FIXED PREMIUM LIFE PRODUCTS

The GMDB for a typical fixed premium product is such that as long as the policy is in force, the death benefit will never be less than the original face amount of the policy, regardless of the actual investment performance of the separate account or the death benefit that would otherwise be generated.

To calculate the GMDB reserve for fixed premium products, a one-year term (OYT) reserve and an attained age level reserve, as defined below, are calculated for each fixed premium variable contract in force. The minimum GMDB is then the greater of the OYT and attained age level reserves.

One-Year Term Reserve

The *one-year term reserve* for a fixed premium variable life contract is equal to the term cost, if any, of the excess of the GMDB over the otherwise payable death benefit, covering a period of one full year from the valuation date,[8] assuming an immediate one-third depreciation in the current value of the assets in the separate accounts, followed by an investment return equal to the assumed investment rate (AIR).

Assuming an investment return equal to the AIR after the immediate one-third depreciation simplifies calculations in the case of an Equitable design product. For Equitable design products, paid-up additions are only purchased if the investment return exceeds the AIR; similarly, negative paid-up additions are only purchased if the investment rate is less than the AIR. Thus, the amount of death benefit provided exclusive of the GMDB remains constant if the investment return equals the AIR. For a policy of the Equitable design, this means that the excess of the GMDB over the otherwise payable death benefit can be calculated as of the date of valuation without any need to project investment results for one year at the AIR. Note that this is not true for products of the New York Life design. Since the death benefit can vary even though the investment return exactly equals the AIR, it is necessary to project the otherwise payable death benefit over the succeeding year, assuming an investment return equal to the AIR, in order to determine the term cost of the excess of this death benefit over the GMDB for the one year period following the date of valuation.

Attained Age Level Reserve

The *attained age level reserve* is equal to the "residue" of the prior year's attained age level reserve for the contract, increased or decreased by the current "payment" as described below. Neither the attained age level reserve nor the residue for any policy can be less than zero.

The "residue" equals the prior year's attained age level reserve for the contract, increased at the valuation interest rate, and decreased for tabular valuation mortality based on the excess, if any, of the GMDB over the death benefit which otherwise would have been in effect during the preceding year. The result is then divided by the tabular probability of survival. The initial residue is zero.

The "payment" is recomputed annually, and is the level annual premium, positive or negative, equal to

$$\frac{A^{GMDB}_{x+t} - A^{SADB}_{x+t} - Residue}{\ddot{a}_{x+t:\overline{n}|}}, \tag{6.1}$$

---

[8] Or, if less, covering the period provided for in the guarantee not otherwise reflected in the separate account reserves.

where the separate account death benefit (SADB) is that which would be payable in the absence of the GMDB, and n is the number of future years for which charges for this risk will be collected under the contract (typically the remaining premium paying period). The SADB is calculated assuming a net investment return of the separate account, chosen by the actuary, which may differ from the AIR but in no event may exceed the maximum valuation rate permitted.

Valuation interest and mortality rates used in computing both the OYT and attained age level reserves need not be the same as those used for the basic reserves, but must conform to the permissible standards for the valuation of life insurance products.

For VUL products, the GMDB reserve is equal to OYT reserves except that the term cost is measured over the life of the GMDB period rather than only one year.[9] No attained age level reserves are calculated for VUL contracts.

It should be noted that calculating the OYT reserve over the life of the GMDB period can result in significantly higher reserves, particularly for single premium contracts, and also makes it more difficult to calculate these reserves.

Example: Fixed Premium Variable Life Equitable Design

Consider a fixed premium variable product of the Equitable design with the following characteristics:

Sex: Male
Issue Age: 35
AIR: 4%
Cash Value and Reserve Basis: Male 80 CSO ANB 4%
Maximum Allowable Statutory Reserve Interest Rate: 6%
Face Amount (GMDB): 100,000
Actual Cash Value at Duration 5: 6,238
Tabular Cash Value at Duration 5: 5,316
Premiums are collected for life

---

[9] To minimize reserve strain, many contracts limit the GMDB period to age 65 or 70.

Values Based on Male 80 CSO ANB:

i	x	$1000A_x$	$\ddot{a}_x$	$1000q_x$
4%	35	246.82	19.5826	2.11
4	36	255.13	19.3667	2.24
4	40	290.81	18.4389	3.02
6%	35	139.51	15.2021	2.11
6	36	146.08	15.0860	2.24
6	40	175.31	14.5695	3.02

$1000q_{39} = 2.79$

Total Amount of Paid-up Additions at Duration 5:

$$\frac{(6,238 - 5,316)}{A_{40}} = \frac{922}{.29081} = 3,170$$

Current Death Benefit (SADB): $100,000 + 3,170 = 103,170$

BASIC RESERVE AT DURATION 5:

$100,000 \cdot {}_5V_{35}^{CRVM} + 3,170 \cdot A_{40}$

$$= 100,000\left(A_{40} - \frac{A_{36}}{\ddot{a}_{36}} \cdot \ddot{a}_{40}\right) + 3,170 \cdot A_{40}$$

$$= 100,000\left(.29081 - \frac{.25513}{19.3667} \cdot 18.4389\right) + (3,170)(.29081)$$

$$= 5,712.12$$

Since the actual cash value of 6,238 is larger than the basic reserve, the separate account liability is equal to the cash value.

GMDB RESERVE AT DURATION 5:

OYT Reserve: Assume cash value drops immediately by one-third to 4,158.67. Purchase negative paid-up additions with $(6,238 - 4,158.67) = 2,079.33$

Amount of Negative PUA's: $\dfrac{2,079.33}{A_{40}} = \dfrac{2,079.33}{.29081} = 7,150.$

Recomputed SADB: $103,170 - 7,150 = 96,020$

Excess of GMDB over death benefit otherwise payable:
$$100,000 - 96,020 = 3,980$$

Cost of excess: $3,980 \cdot \dfrac{q_{40}}{1+i} = 3,980\left(\dfrac{.00303}{1.06}\right) = 11.34$

Note that 6% interest has been used to calculate the OYT reserve, although the company has used a more conservative rate in the calculation of the policy's basic reserve.

Attained age level reserve: Assume previous year's attained age level reserve was 100. Also assume that the actual death benefit exceeded the GMDB during the previous year.

Residue: $\dfrac{100(1.06) - 0}{1 - q_{39}} = \dfrac{106}{.99721} = 106.30$

The tabular mortality deduction is zero, since the actual death benefit exceeded the GMDB during the previous year.

Payment: $\dfrac{100,000 \cdot A_{40} - 103,170 \cdot A_{40} - 106.30}{\ddot{a}_{40}}$

$$= \dfrac{-3170(.17531) - 106.30}{14.5695} = -45.44$$

New attained age level reserve: $106.30 - 45.44 = 60.86$

Note that 6% interest has been used in the calculation of the attained age level reserve, even though the basic reserves have been calculated at 4%.

The GMDB reserve is the larger of the OYT and the attained age level reserve, which is 60.86 in this case.

If the average death benefit in force during the previous year had been 95,000 were it not for the existence of the GMDB, the residue in the above example would have been

$$\frac{100(1.06) - (100,000-95,000)q_{39}}{1 - q_{39}} = 92.31,$$

rather than 106.30 as developed previously.

GMDB RESERVES: ANNUITY PRODUCTS

As previously mentioned, most variable annuity contracts offer a return of premium death benefit guarantee. This involves some risk to the insurer, in that the death benefit may exceed the statutory reserves when account values have decreased.

Additionally, many variable annuities now offer enhanced death benefits. These may be GMDBs which ratchet up at the end of the surrender charge period, such that the minimum death benefit is then the larger of the premium paid or the account value at the point in time when the surrender charge grades off. Other enhanced death benefits available include annual ratchets, and ratchets which are equal to the premium paid accumulated at a stated interest rate.

Virtually all insurers hold a GMDB reserve for their variable annuity contracts with such provisions. Reserves are typically calculated as the one-year term cost of the shortfall, with or without a 1/3 drop in the current asset value, or expressed as a percentage of the account value in a simplifying calculation. Percentages of the account value may vary depending on the type of fund, reflecting the relative volatility.

An alternative approach is to allocate an annual contribution, equal to a percentage of the account value which varies by duration, to the GMDB reserve. Under this approach, any death benefits in excess of the basic reserve are deducted from the GMDB reserve.

EXERCISES

1. A fixed premium variable life contract had an original level death benefit of $10,000. Due to favorable investment performance in the separate account, the death benefit as of the 5th policy anniversary is $15,000. Ignoring the GMDB reserve and the cash value floor, what is the formula for the reserve at that time for each of the following contracts?

    (a) New York Life design
    (b) Equitable design

2. Fixed premium variable products typically have long-term minimum death benefit guarantees, whereas flexible premium products do not. What would be the reserve implications of guaranteeing, under a flexible premium product, that the death benefit will be at least a level $10,000 for the first 10 policy years, under the condition that the policyholder pay a minimum required premium annually during this time period?

CHAPTER SEVEN

MISCELLANEOUS RESERVES

This chapter deals with the calculation of reserves which are held in addition to the basic policy reserves. Some of these reserves are held for supplemental benefits which are sold with, or as an inherent part of, the basic life insurance policy. Others are additional liabilities associated with the basic policy benefits, which may be required due to the product design or the type of basic policy reserve used by the company. Also discussed in this chapter are basic reserve considerations for lapse-supported policies and last-to-die policies.

Many miscellaneous reserves tend to be quite small in relation to the reserves for the basic policy benefits. Several of these miscellaneous reserves are not only relatively insignificant, but are also quite complicated to calculate on an exact basis, and hence, in practice, tend to be calculated using considerably less precise techniques than for the basic policy benefit reserves. Sometimes single average ages are used, and a single set of reserve factors may be used for a wide range of policy forms which would theoretically require calculation of separate factors. It is generally felt that the use of gross approximations is acceptable for many of these reserves; however, the valuation actuary, as always, has the responsibility of certifying that the reserves make good and sufficient provision for the unmatured policy obligations, and should be able to prove to his or her own satisfaction that the use of such approximations will not be significantly less than the exact reserve. Furthermore, given that U.S. companies must use Federally Prescribed Tax Reserves to determine taxable income, the valuation actuary must also be prepared to show that such approximations do not significantly overstate reserve liabilities, resulting in lower taxable income. This is not to imply that the use of approximations is unacceptable for these reserves. However, it is up to the valuation actuary to review the approximations from time to time to be satisfied as to their continued acceptability.

There are several methods used in practice to calculate reserves for many of these benefits, with the method chosen dependent upon each company's available data. The methods illustrated in the following pages are not necessarily more acceptable or more accurate than other methods which are in common use.

DEFICIENCY RESERVES

The basic reserve definition is $_tV = A_{x+t} - P \cdot \ddot{a}_{x+t}$, the present value of future benefits less the present value of future net premiums.

However, what if gross premiums are less than the valuation net premiums? Is it prudent to subtract the present value of future net premiums when the policyholder will be remitting less than the annual net premium to the insurance company?

Deficiency reserves are reserves which may be required in addition to basic policy reserves when the gross premium is below a certain level as described below.

U.S. Requirements

Before the 1976 changes, the Standard Valuation Law required deficiency reserves if the gross premium for a policy were less than the valuation net premium actually used.

Deficiency reserves were subject to criticism for several reasons:

(1) Suppose that a company strengthens reserves by reducing the valuation interest rate from 3.5% to 3%, and suppose the gross premiums for a policy are greater than the net premiums at 3.5%, but less at 3%. Reserve strengthening would cause the basic policy reserve to increase. Yet, as a result of lowering the valuation rate, deficiency reserves would be required.

(2) Although reserve strengthening occurs rarely in practice, this example illustrates that the prior law sometimes required companies with conservative reserve bases to hold deficiency reserves

even though they would not have been necessary if a more liberal basis had been adopted.

(3) Deficiency reserves have not been allowed as a tax reserve in the U.S.

The 1976 amendments to the Standard Valuation Law removed any explicit reference to deficiency reserves. Instead, basic policy reserves are required to be increased under certain circumstances. Under the 1976 amendments, if the gross premium for a policy is less than the valuation net premium calculated using the valuation method actually used, but using the *minimum* standards of mortality and interest, then the required total reserve is the greater of (a) or (b), defined as

(a) the reserve calculated according to the method, mortality table, and interest rate actually used for the policy, and

(b) the reserve calculated by the method actually used for the policy, but using the minimum valuation standards of mortality and interest,[1] and replacing the valuation net premium by the actual gross premium in each year that the actual gross premium is less than the valuation net premium.

Although the Standard Valuation Law now makes no explicit reference to deficiency reserves, the excess of reserves described in (b) over those described in (a) is often referred to as a deficiency reserve.[2] This terminology is followed throughout the remainder of this chapter.

The important changes in the new definition are that (1) regardless of the basis of mortality and interest actually used in the basic reserves, the test for premium deficiency is now performed against a net premium calculated using the minimum allowable standards of mortality and interest, and (2) where the test reveals any deficiencies, the policy gets credit for the excess of the actual basic reserve over the reserve calculated using the minimum basis of mortality and interest, and this credit is used to offset any deficiency reserves which would otherwise be required. These changes generally eliminate many of the inequities which occur when a company strengthens reserves, and when two

---

[1] According to Actuarial Guideline I, the minimum standards in effect at the date of policy issue.

[2] And is so treated by the Internal Revenue Service. The Valuation Model Regulation, discussed later in this chapter, also defines deficiency reserves in this manner.

companies use different reserving bases for essentially similar policies. Note, however, that both the test for premium deficiency and the calculation of adjusted reserves utilize the actual valuation **method** used by the company. In particular, if a company were to strengthen reserves by switching from a CRVM to some other basis, the new definition might not offer complete relief from deficiency reserves.

The additional reserve required under the new definition can be defined by the following terminal reserve formula for a whole life plan.

$$_tV_x^{Def} = \left(A_{x+t}^M - G \cdot \ddot{a}_{x+t}^M\right) - \left(A_{x+t} - P \cdot \ddot{a}_{x+t}\right)$$

$$= \left(A_{x+t}^M - P^M \cdot \ddot{a}_{x+t}^M\right) + (P^M - G) \cdot \ddot{a}_{x+t}^M - (A_{x+t} - P \cdot \ddot{a}_{x+t}) \quad (7.1)$$

$$= (P^M - G) \cdot \ddot{a}_{x+t}^M - [(A_{x+t} - P \cdot \ddot{a}_{x+t}) - (A_{x+t}^M - P^M \cdot \ddot{a}_{x+t}^M)],$$

where G is the gross premium (assumed here to be less than P^M), P is the valuation net premium, M denotes the minimum standards of mortality and interest, and symbols without M denote the mortality and interest basis used by the company to calculate basic reserves. Note that $_tV_x^{Def}$ may not be less than zero.

The first term of Formula (7.1) equals the deficiency reserve required before 1976. If a policy is valued using the minimum standards of mortality and interest, and if the valuation net premium exceeds the gross premium, then the deficiency reserve required under the 1976 law would exactly equal the deficiency reserve under the prior law.

Deficiency reserves do not follow the usual pattern of premium paying life reserves in that they generally begin at their maximum value[3] at issue and decrease with time. The initial deficiency reserve may be much greater than the initial premium for a given policy. (See Figure 7.1 on page 115.) Because of the resulting surplus strain, actuaries try to design products which either do not require or which minimize deficiency reserves.[4]

---

[3] This may not be true for policies with modified reserve bases, or for policies with unlevel premiums.

[4] This is particularly true since deficiency reserves are not allowable tax reserves in the U.S.

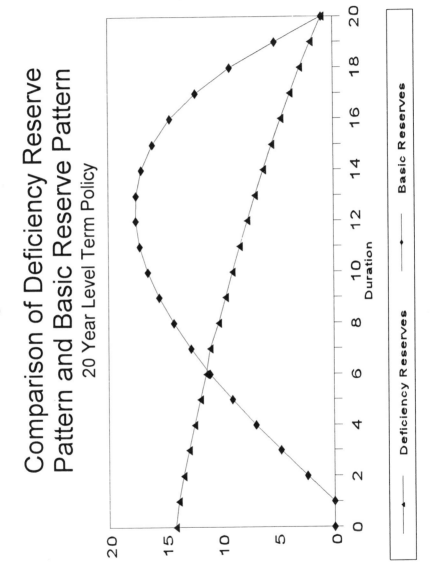

Figure 7.1

Comparison of Deficiency Reserve
Pattern and Basic Reserve Pattern
20 Year Level Term Policy

Practical Considerations of Deficiency Reserves

The gross premium used in the calculation of deficiency reserves under the 1976 amendments to the Standard Valuation Law is the total annualized gross premium for the base policy, including modal loading and policy fee. Although premiums for benefits and riders are not allowed to be used in calculation of deficiencies for the base policy, sufficiencies in one benefit are allowed to offset deficiencies in another benefit, including the base policy. For example, deficiencies in a whole life policy may be reduced by any sufficiencies in a term rider.

Because of these complications, the most common means of calculating these reserves is by the seriatim method[5], with either the minimum required net premium, or the amount of deficiency maintained in the valuation record. The inclusion of policy fees in most policies makes it impossible to use factor type approaches without having to make critical assumptions as to the average policy size. The potential significant size of deficiency reserves, and the fact that they frequently start out at their maximum value combine to cause most companies to calculate these reserves on a fairly exact basis rather than relying on crude approximations.

As discussed above, the 1976 amendments require companies to recalculate the basic policy reserves for policies with deficient premiums, using the gross premium in lieu of the valuation net premium under the policy. Because this could involve fairly complicated reserve calculations based upon first principles, many companies continue to calculate additional required reserves using the old technique, although substituting the minimum basis of mortality and interest. As discussed above, this produces the exact answer in the typical case where the policy is reserved at the minimum basis of mortality and interest. Using this method, the mid-year deficiency reserve for an n-pay-life policy is

$$(P - G)\left[\frac{a_{x+t-1:\overline{n-t}|} + \ddot{a}_{x+t:\overline{n-t}|}}{2}\right] \approx (P - G)\left[\frac{\ddot{a}_{x+t:\overline{n-t}|}}{1 + \frac{i}{2}}\right], \qquad (7.2)$$

where P and G are the net and gross premiums, respectively.

---

[5] That is, on a policy-by-policy basis, as opposed to using a grouping approach and applying factors.

In practice, the actual formula used may be much more complicated than that given above, although the basic principle will be the same. Common complications include the utilization of modified reserve methods which grade from one basis to another, producing varying net premiums, and the existence of additional benefits whose sufficiencies which may be used to offset the deficiencies of the base policy.[6]

Deficiency Reserves for Renewable Term Policies

Until the mid 1970's, it was common practice in the life insurance industry to consider renewable term policies as a series of separate policies for purposes of calculating deficiency reserves. Most companies only held reserves for the deficiencies during the current period of level premiums. According to this view, deficiency reserves would never be required for an annually renewable term (ART) policy. As a practical matter, this practice did not threaten company solvency, as term rates were, for the most part, in excess of net valuation premiums.

Then in the late 1970's and early 1980's, ART rates fell as new product types and nonsmoker discounts were introduced. State regulators became concerned that rates below the valuation net premium level were being guaranteed without a corresponding deficiency reserve. Several states introduced requirements that renewable term products be viewed as ongoing policies for purposes of deficiency reserve calculations.

It soon developed that there were two ways of looking at valuation premiums for renewable term policies:

(1) The *unitary* method considers the entire stream of future gross premiums and develops a set of valuation net premiums which are proportional. This method follows from a literal reading of the Standard Valuation Law, which requires that the valuation net premiums for a policy be proportional to the gross premiums.

(2) The *term* method looks separately at the gross premiums for each renewal period and develops separate, independent sets of valuation net premiums within each period.

---

[6] This case is particularly complicated when the premium paying period of the benefit is less than that of the base policy.

Although the unitary method may appear to be more in line with the Standard Valuation Law, it quickly fell into disfavor with regulators. Because this method considers the entire stream of gross premiums, regardless how low the premiums are in the early durations, it is always possible to avoid deficiency reserves by setting the gross premiums at the extreme older attained ages high enough to offset any deficiencies at the younger ages. In 1984 the NAIC adopted Actuarial Guideline IV, which was applicable to term policies without cash values which were valued using the 1958 CSO table. For applicable policies, Actuarial Guideline IV required that term method reserves be set up for the current period of level premiums, and that additional reserves be established if future guaranteed premiums were less than valuation net premiums, calculated according to a special basis specified in the Guideline.

In 1995 the NAIC adopted the Valuation of Life Insurance Policies Model Regulation, which clarifies both basic and deficiency reserve treatment of all policies with nonlevel premiums or benefits.[7] The Valuation Model Regulation defines a *contract segmentation method* as follows:

- The policy is divided into *contract segments*, by taking the ratio

$$G_t = \frac{GP_{x+k+t}}{GP_{x+k+t-1}}$$

where GP_{x+t} is the guaranteed[8] gross premium per thousand of face amount for year t, ignoring policy fees if they are level for the premium paying period of the policy, and comparing it to

$$R_t = \frac{q_{x+k+t}}{q_{x+k+t-1}}$$

where q_{x+t} is the valuation mortality rate applicable for deficiency reserves in policy year t. Each time G_t is greater than R_t a new

---

[7] Traditional policies are subject to the requirements of the Valuation Model Regulation if the premiums or benefits guaranteed by the contract are nonlevel. Applicability of the Valuation Model Regulation to Universal Life policies is discussed in Chapter 4.

[8] Many policies are issued with a set of current premiums which are intended to be charged to the policyholder, but with a separate set of higher guaranteed premiums. The company reserves the right to change the current premiums if expected future experience significantly changes at some point in the future. Under the Valuation Model Regulation, contract segment determination is based upon the guaranteed premium scale. It should be noted, however, that New York Regulation 147, which otherwise largely parallels Valuation Model Regulation, requires segments to be based upon the current premium scale.

segment is created. Thus, for the typical ten year renewable term policy with guaranteed premiums increasing every ten years, the contract segments would be equal to each ten year period of level guaranteed premiums. Note that for purposes of this calculation R_t may be increased or decreased by up to 1% in any policy year, to avoid situations where rounding causes new segments to be created.

- Basic reserves are calculated by calculating basic valuation net premiums separately for each segment such that within a segment they are level as a percentage of the gross premiums, and such that at the beginning of the segment, the present value of the net premiums within the segment equals the present value of benefits within that segment. A CRVM expense allowance is permitted for the first segment only.[9]

  Thus, for the typical ten year renewable term policy, basic reserves using the contract segmentation method are essentially calculated using the term method, with CRVM reserves during the first ten year period, and net level reserves for each of the remaining ten year periods. Thus, the basic reserve has been described as having a "humpbacked" shape (see Figure 7.2 on page 120), with the reserve at zero at the beginning of each segment, rising to a maximum near the middle of the segment, and descending to zero at the end of the segment.

- The Valuation Model Regulation requires that basic reserves for the contract be equal to the greater of unitary reserves and segmented reserves for each policy duration. *n*-year renewable term policies with non-deficient guaranteed premiums are exempted from this unitary requirement. Also, there are special exemptions for attained age YRT policies.

- Deficiency reserves are calculated as in the 1976 amendments, using guaranteed gross premiums instead of the net premiums, and taking credit for any sufficiencies due to conservative reserving methodology. Additionally, there is a five year safe harbor, such that, if the length of the first segment is five years or less, then gross premiums need not be substituted for net premiums for

---

[9] Additionally, reserves must be established for any unusual guaranteed cash values as defined in the Valuation Model Regulation, with the effect that these unusual cash values must essentially be reserved as pure endowments.

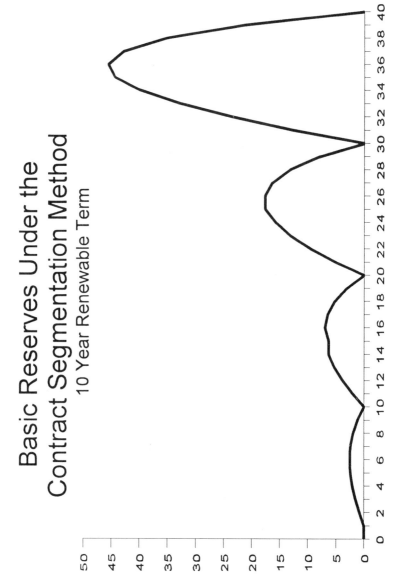

Figure 7.2

Basic Reserves Under the
Contract Segmentation Method
10 Year Renewable Term

that period, even if the gross premiums are deficient. Thus, for the typical 5 year renewable term policy, if the premium for the initial period only is deficient, no deficiency reserves are required. To use this safe harbor, the actuary must annually submit an opinion that the reserves held for all such policies are adequate.

• The Valuation Model Regulation allows the use of new, up-dated selection factors in the calculation of basic reserves. For deficiency reserves even lower selection factors are allowed.

The Contract Segmentation Method is the result of long negotiations between state regulators and industry groups, and as of July 1996, only New York had adopted a modified version of the Regulation, with adoption in several other states considered likely in the near future. While clearing up the reserving of policies with nonlevel premiums and benefits, the Regulation is very complex (even more complex than would be inferred from the brief summary above) and has many unexpected consequences. For example, reserves for decreasing term policies, which are frequently sold as mortgage protection insurance, used to be calculated using simple CRVM methods. However, the decreasing face amount causes a number of segments to be created, greatly complicating the reserve calculations for these policies.

Canadian Practice for Renewable Term Policies

The Canadian Institute of Actuaries' (CIA) Valuation Technique Paper No. 2, "The Valuation of Individual Renewable Term Insurance," deals with the same topic as Actuarial Guideline IV. CIA Valuation Technique Paper No. 2 also deals with recommendations regarding mortality assumptions and reentry assumptions for these products. The summary below is taken from that paper.

(1) Benefits, premiums and expenses should be valued to the end of the benefit period, not to an earlier renewal date.

(2) The excess of heaped commissions at a renewal date over normal renewal commissions may be treated in the same fashion as issue expenses.

(3) A method of calculating the net valuation premium when the gross premiums are not level, for the purpose of determining the maximum deferrable issue expenses, is described in the document.

(4) Lapse rates can be expected to show a sudden (temporary) increase when premium rates increase at a renewal date. In general, healthy lives are more likely to lapse their policies at renewal than unhealthy lives, the net effect being a deterioration in mortality for the remaining lives.

(5) In valuing re-entry products, it is necessary to make an assumption about the percentage of policyholders who will requalify for select rates at each renewal date. This percentage is referred to as the "Re-entry Proportion."

Ignoring anti-selective lapses, the mortality for the group of policyholders as a whole should resemble the normal select and ultimate mortality one would expect from a single scale product. For example, the mortality rate in the sixth policy year for the total group will be $q_{[x]+5}$, and the gross premium will be

$$RP \times GPS + (1-RP) \times GPU, \qquad (7.3)$$

where RP is the Re-entry Proportion, GRP is the select (preferred) renewal rate, and GPU is the ultimate (guaranteed) renewal rate.

By using this technique, the valuation actuary no longer has to make an explicit assumption regarding the mortality of those that do not requalify for select rates. Instead, an assumption with respect to the Re-entry Proportion is required.

Alternative Minimum Reserves for Universal Life

The NAIC Model Universal Life Regulation requires that *alternative minimum reserves* (AMR's) be established if the guaranteed gross premium is less than the corresponding valuation net premium in the case of a fixed premium Universal Life policy, and when the policy fund guarantees are "too liberal" in relation to the valuation basis in the case of a flexible premium Universal Life policy.

These reserves are covered in detail in Chapter 4. However, these reserves are analogous to deficiency reserves, and many of the same considerations apply. For example, the minimum basis of mortality and interest are used to test for AMR's, but the company must use same valuation method as for the basic policy reserves.

ACCIDENTAL DEATH BENEFIT

Reserves for Accidental Death Benefit (ADB) are usually calculated using the accidental death tables mentioned in the Standard Valuation Law (the 1959 ADB Table for 1966 and later issues) along with permissible levels of mortality and interest determined by the basic policy type.[10] The Canadian valuation laws are silent as to the valuation bases for ADB, as they are silent for life benefits, and it is the actuary's responsibility that the method and assumptions are appropriate and that the reserve makes good and sufficient provision for the liabilities as required by Canadian law.

In practice, in both countries the method used to calculate ADB reserves is normally similar to the method used to calculate basic policy reserves. A company could use either a mean or mid-terminal approach for these extra reserves.

The mean reserve for an m-pay, n-year benefit would be

$$_t MV_x^{ad} = \frac{_{t-1}V_x^{ad} + {_t}V_x^{ad} + P_x^{ad}}{2}, \tag{7.4}$$

where

$$_t V_x^{ad} = \frac{1000(M_{x+t}^{ad} - M_{x+n}^{ad}) - P_x^{ad}(N_{x+t} - N_{x+m})}{D_{x+t}}, \tag{7.5}$$

$$P_x^{ad} = \frac{1000(M_x^{ad} - M_{x+n}^{ad})}{N_x - N_{x+m}}, \tag{7.6}$$

and

$$M_x^{ad} = \sum v \cdot q_x^{ad} \cdot D_x. \tag{7.7}$$

Many approximations are in use for ADB reserves. Some companies develop factors based on age grouping, and it is not uncommon to group plans, even when the premium payment periods are not identical.

---

[10] That is, the permissible mortality table and interest rate is the same as allowed for the base policy.

Many home service companies market life policies with ADB (and other benefits) as an inherent part of the policy, without a separately identifiable gross premium for the benefit. The calculation of ADB reserves (or reserves for any other inherent benefit) is particularly complicated when the gross premiums for the policy extend beyond the ADB benefit period.

Calculating ADB reserves assuming payment of net premiums beyond the benefit period is awkward and presents practical difficulties. However, if a portion of the gross premiums is assumed to pay for the ADB benefit only during the life of that benefit, the remaining gross premium, which pays for the basic policy benefit, is an increasing amount, which means that the reserves for the base policy should be based on an increasing premium. It is probably safe to say that few companies, if any, a recalculating ADB reserves in this theoretically justifiable way. It is the responsibility of the valuation actuary that the actual method used is reasonable, and methods which assume payment of the ADB net premium beyond the benefit period should be avoided, if practical to do so.

ADB is commonly available on many Universal Life products, sometimes with a scale of ADB cost of insurance charges based on issue age, and sometimes with a set based on attained age. In the case of charges based on issue age, reserve considerations would be identical to those for the same benefit on a traditional whole life product. In the case of a scale which varies by attained age, reserve considerations are much the same as for a traditional ART product. In this latter case, if the slope of the ADB cost of insurance charges bears a reasonable resemblance to the ADB valuation table, and if those charges generally exceed net premiums based on that table, a reasonable and commonly used approximation is to hold the unearned portion, or one-half, of the most recent month's charges for the benefit. Alternatively, monthly net ADB premiums could be calculated and used to determine the reserve.

DISABILITY WAIVER OF PREMIUM BENEFITS

The Standard Valuation Law requires this benefit to be valued using the tables of Period 2 disablement rates of the 1952 Disability Study of the Society of Actuaries. For active lives, this table is combined with a mortality table and interest rate permitted for calculating the basic policy reserves.

The Canadian valuation laws are silent as to valuation bases for disability benefits. Once again, the actuary is guided by the requirement that the valuation assumptions be appropriate and that the reserve made good and sufficient provision for the liabilities.

Active Life Reserves

A question which needs to be addressed in both premium and reserve calculations for disability waiver benefits is what premium is to be waived on a disability claim. Should it be the gross premium or the net premium for the basic policy benefits? Should it include the disability premium? What about other benefits, such as ADB?

Most companies continue to pay commissions and policyholder dividends whether or not premiums are being waived. In this case, the disability reserve should be set up to provide for waiver of the gross, rather than the net premium under the policy.

In practice, most companies also waive the disability premium, as well as the premium for other benefits such as ADB. Active life reserves may be calculated assuming that only the basic premium is waived. Then, the ratio of the average premium for ADB to the average base policy premium, and the percentage of policies having ADB, may be applied to the disability reserve to approximate the reserve required to waive the premium for the ADB premium.

Practical considerations in calculating active life disability waiver of premium reserves are similar to those for ADB. As with ADB, many approximations are used in practice, and companies tend to use plan grouping rather than calculating exact waiver of premium factors for each plan of insurance. Also as with ADB, waiver of premium is found as an inherent benefit on many home service policies, and once again the actuary should avoid, if practical, net premiums for such a benefit which are assumed to extend beyond the benefit period. Finally, the reserves should reflect the premiums. On ART the benefit is an increasing amount.

Waiver of premium is another common benefit offered on many Universal Life policies. Two types of waiver of premium are generally available:

(1) *Waiver of the Cost of Insurance* waives the total cost of insurance and expense charges for the basic policy, and usually for all riders as well.

(2) *Waiver of Planned Premium* waives the specified premium amount on a monthly basis.

The primary difference is that Waiver of the Cost of Insurance stops deductions from the fund, and Waiver of Planned Premium actually increments the fund by a fixed amount on a monthly basis. It is possible, if unlikely, that this specified amount could be less than the monthly deductions for a particular policy. To avoid this situation, a number of companies have developed riders which waive the greater of the two amounts.

If the Waiver of Planned Premium rates are on an issue age basis, reserve calculations are the same as those for a traditional whole life policy. If the Waiver of Cost of Insurance rates are on an attained age basis, reserve calculations are similar to those for a similar ART policy, although much more complicated theoretically, since the future premiums to be waived are not known.[11] If the rates for either type of waiver are on an attained age basis, if the slope of the rates is similar to the slope of the disability table used for valuation, and if the rates per 100 waived are not less than the corresponding valuation table rates, it is reasonable to hold the unearned portion, or one-half, of the most recent month's charge for the benefit. Alternatively, net valuation premiums can be calculated in this latter case.

Disabled Life Reserves

Reserves for disabled lives consist of liabilities for four types of claim status:

(1) Approved claims
(2) In course of settlement (pending approval)
(3) Resisted
(4) Incurred but unreported

The last three are considered policy claim liabilities.[12] Liabilities for claims in course of settlement and for resisted claims are determined based upon actual data as of the valuation dates. Liabilities for claims incurred but unreported are generally based on factors derived from prior years' experience. Factors are developed which may be applied to claims approved during the year, outstanding disability benefits, or some other known item.

---

[11] Ignoring the effects of the minimum death benefit cash value corridor, it is conservative to calculate these amounts under the assumption that the amount at risk will remain constant.

[12] Although incurred but unreported is often split into a liability portion consisting of amounts due prior to the valuation date and a reserve portion based on the present value of future amounts due.

Valuation factors for approved claims usually consist of disabled life annuities based on the tables mentioned in the Standard Valuation Law (or the Canadian actuary's best judgment) together with an appropriate valuation interest rate. Approved claims are then valued by applying these factors to the amount being waived. The expression for mean reserves for the waiver of 1 per year, as specified in the Society's 1952 Disability Study, is

$$\ddot{a}_{[x+.5]+n-.5:\overline{t-.5}|}, \qquad (7.8)$$

where x is the insurance age attained on the policy anniversary before disability, n is the policy year of disability, and t is the number of years which benefits run as measured from the policy anniversary in the year of valuation.

Since the valuation depends on age at disability, duration since disability, and number of years to run, and since there are relatively few claims compared to the active life in force, a seriatim valuation is normally used.

DISABILITY AND DEATH OF PAYOR BENEFITS

The typical *payor benefit* waives premiums to a child's age 21 or 25 upon the death or disability of the parent. The theoretical reserve for payor benefits is complicated as there are two lives involved, and, in the case of the disability payor benefit, both death and disability must be considered. This coverage is essentially decreasing term, and small or negative reserves are to be expected, so approximations are normally used.

Usually the mortality of the child is ignored when determining the reserves. As the terminal reserves for juvenile active payor benefits are often negative, many companies hold one-half of the gross annual premium as an approximate unearned premium reserve.

The reserve after the death of the payor is an annuity for the number of future premiums payable under the terms of the benefit. This is usually approximated by using an annuity-certain and ignoring the mortality of the child.[13] The result held upon the disability of the payor would be the regular disabled life waiver reserve for the remaining period during which premiums

---

[13] However, in the U.S., this reserve may not qualify as a tax reserve unless the mortality of the child is recognized.

can be waived. Again, the mortality of the child is often ignored when calculating these reserves.

NONDEDUCTION OF DEFERRED FRACTIONAL PREMIUMS AT DEATHS

As discussed previously, the required additional reserve for this benefit is equal to a term reserve, over the term of the policy's premium paying period, for an amount of insurance equal to

$$\frac{m-1}{2m} \cdot P^{(m)}, \tag{7.9}$$

where $P^{(m)}$ is the net premium for the basic plan.

One common method of approximating this liability is given below, under the assumptions that the distribution of mode of premium payment is the same for all durations, plans, and ages.

For each reserve basis, select a few major plans still in the premium paying period. For each major plan (or for selected age groupings within a plan), the following steps are taken:

(1) Calculate the following totals for all issue ages and durations combined: amounts of insurance (S^{tot}), gross annual premiums[14] (G^{tot}), net annual premiums (P^{tot}), and base plan reserves (V^{tot}).

(2) Calculate an average gross premium ($\bar{G}$) and an average net annual premium ($\bar{P}$) per 1000, by dividing the total gross premium and total net premium by the total amount of insurance from the results in Step 1. That is $\bar{G} = \frac{G^{tot}}{S^{tot}}$ and $\bar{P} = \frac{P^{tot}}{S^{tot}}$. Use these average premiums to select an average issue age $\bar{x}$ based on a comparison with actual gross and net premiums for the plan.

(3) Determine an average basic plan reserve per 1000 of insurance ($\bar{V}$) by dividing the total reserve, V^{tot}, by the total amount of insurance, S^{tot}, from Step 1.

---

[14] Exclusive of substandard extras.

(4) From the average issue age in Step 2, and the average reserve in Step 3, determine an average duration $\bar{t}$.

(5) From the average issue age and duration, determine an average term reserve factor for the term of the basic plan's premium paying period, $_{\bar{t}}V^1_{\overline{x:n|}}$, where n is the original premium paying period of the plan (20 for 20-pay-life, etc.). Note that for whole life and full-pay term plans, Steps 2, 4, and 5 may be omitted and the average reserve factor determined in Step 3 can be used directly.

(6) Multiply the term reserve factor in Step 5 for each main plan by the total amount of basic net annual premium in force for that plan from Step 1.

After obtaining the above factors for each main plan, two final steps remain:

(1) Sum the net annual premiums obtained in Step 1 and the products obtained in Step 6 to obtain totals for all main plans combined for each reserve basis; denote these totals by $\sum\limits_{plans} P^{tot}$ and $\sum\limits_{plans} \left(P^{tot} \cdot {}_{\bar{t}}V^1_{\overline{x:n|}} \right)$.

(2) From these totals obtain an average nondeduction reserve fac-tor per dollar of net annual premium, $\dfrac{\sum P^{tot} \cdot {}_{\bar{t}}V^1_{\overline{x:n|}}}{\sum P^{tot}}$. This factor is usually applied to the total net deferred premiums for all plans of the reserve basis, and is also used in determining the nondeduction reserve for ADB and disability benefits.

Note that in practice, due to the small size of the resulting reserve, the above factor may be applied to a range of reserve bases "close to" the one for which the factor was developed. Simplifying assumptions are often made, especially if the value of endowment and limited pay life is relatively low. As the reserve declines with increasing interest rates, it is generally conservative to continue using an older factor as newer plans are introduced at higher valu-ation rates. However, it is the responsibility of the actuary to be assured that the nondeduction factor used continues to be adequate as the mix of business shifts.

Surrender Values in Excess of Reserves

In the event that the surrender value on any policy or contract in the U.S. exceeds the reserve otherwise required or held, then an additional reserve equal in amount to such excess must be established in Exhibit 8G of the annual statement. The need for the additional reserve is infrequent and isolated, generally arising from errors, since it is unlikely that surrender values would be designed intentionally to exceed reserves on any policy or contract.

Wightman[15] indicates that the additional reserve, if any, should be determined on a policy-by-policy basis, as opposed to a determination in the aggregate on all policies and contracts combined. In other words, there should be no offsetting of policies and contracts with reserves greater than surrender values against those with reserves less than surrender values in arriving at the additional reserves. This interpretation appears to be commonly accepted within the industry.

CANADIAN LAPSE-SUPPORTED POLICIES

A type of product that was introduced in Canada in the early 1980's is a life insurance policy providing level death benefits for level premium that has little or no cash value for extended periods of time after issue.[16] As mentioned previously, lapses are explicitly recognized in the development of reserves in Canada. For a product with level premiums and no cash values, the higher the ultimate rate of lapsation the smaller the reserve would be.

Also as previously mentioned, interest assumptions are no longer prescribed as they are in the U.S. Therefore the reserves for a level premium term-to-100 or zero cash value whole life product will be quite sensitive to the assumed level of investment return. Concern developed in Canada that reserves were being established for this type of product which depended on a significant level of ultimate lapsation in order for the reserves to be adequate.

To address this concern, the Canadian Institute of Actuaries developed a valuation technique paper regarding the valuation of lapse-supported policies.

---

[15] E.C. Wightman, *Life Insurance Statements and Accounts*, Life Office Management Association, 1952, p. 191.

[16] Such products are generally not allowed in the U.S., although there has been an increasing amount of discussion over whether changes should be made to allow such products.

This valuation technique paper cautions the valuation actuary to recognize that the level of reserves on lapse-supported products can be very sensitive to changes in assumptions, particularly lapses and interest rates. The actuary should therefore test the sensitivity of reserves to changes in assumptions and take particular care in selecting assumptions for which a small change could have a major impact on reserves.

The following seven points are taken from the Canadian Institute of Actuaries' Valuation Technique Paper No. 1, "The Valuation of Lapse-Supported Products":

(1) In valuing lapse-supported products, the two most significant assumptions are normally lapses and interest. The level of reserves can be very sensitive to changes in these assumptions, and the valuation actuary should test this sensitivity.

(2) It is appropriate in most cases to assume that Ultimate Lapse Rates will be greater than zero (but see items (5) and (6) below).

(3) It is rarely appropriate to use an Ultimate Lapse Rate for valuation in excess of 3%.

(4) The presence of certain policy features or marketing considerations requires an Ultimate Lapse Rate for valuation less than 3%; these factors include
  (a) sophistication of the market (greater sophistication is likely to result in lower lapse rates);
  (b) high quality sale;
  (c) levelized commission structure;
  (d) large amounts of insurance;
  (e) degree of loss to the policyholder on lapse (lapse rates are likely to decrease as the benefit given up on lapse increases);
  (f) the presence of a "Cliff";[17]
  (g) the existence of a Return of Premium rider.

(5) The valuation lapse rate should grade to zero over a period of years prior to attainment of a Cliff, and should normally be zero for a short period immediately preceding.

(6) In the absence of any cash values, lapse rates should be assumed to be zero after a policy becomes paid-up.

(7) Return of Premium riders have the potential for lower Ultimate Lapse Rates than any other lapse-supported product currently

---

[17] A Cliff is a sudden and significant increase in the level of non-forfeiture values available.

being sold. The comments made about Cliffs in item (5) also apply to Return of Premium riders, but the period of zero valuation lapse rates should normally be longer, and the grading of the valuation lapse rate to zero should normally start earlier.

The points in this paper should be considered as guidelines, but more conservative assumptions are appropriate if indicated by company experience or professional judgement. For example, recent industry data suggests that the 3% ultimate lapse rate referenced in the third point above may be too liberal in many cases, as a number of companies have experienced rates of 2% or below by the 8th duration.

The experience in Canada illustrates the importance of investment return and lapse assumptions on reserve levels. For many products these two assumptions are considered the most important in pricing an insurance product, yet in the U.S. the interest rate is specified and lapses are ignored in determining reserves according to the prescribed reserving methods.

LAST-TO-DIE POLICIES

In recent years there has been renewed interest in *last-to-die*, or *last-survivor* policies. These policies pay a death benefit at the *later* death of two (or more) insureds.

Last-to-die policies are of two types:

(1) *Traditional* policies either pay an extra, reduced, death benefit, or become paid-up at the first death. After the first death, the cash values for these policies are calculated using single life values for the remaining life.

(2) *Frasier-type* policies[18] have no change in status at the first death. Cash values are calculated independently of whether a death has occurred.

Reserves for last-to-die policies[19] vary according to the policy type.

---

[18] After William Frasier, who first described this type of policy in an article in *The Actuary*.

[19] This discussion applies to reserve calculations, and not to cost of insurance rate calculations for Universal Life-type last-to-die policies, for which many methods are in use (including the use of single life COI rates).

Reserves for Traditional Policies

For traditional policies, the reserve before the first death should take into account any benefits upon the first death, and should also take into account that both insureds are alive at the time of valuation. For a traditional policy which becomes paid up at the first death of (x) and (y), the terminal reserve at t is

$$A_{\overline{x+t:y+t}} - P \cdot \ddot{a}_{x+t:y+t}, \tag{7.10}$$

where P is the net premium. For a traditional policy which is not paid-up at the first death, but which pays an additional 20% of the death benefit at the first death and 100% at the second, the terminal reserve is

$$A_{\overline{x+t:y+t}} + .20 \cdot A_{x+t:y+t} - P \cdot \ddot{a}_{\overline{x+t:y+t}}, \tag{7.11}$$

where P is the net premium (different, of course, than the one in (7.10)).

After the first death, the reserve is based on functions of the remaining life. Assuming the prior death of (x), the terminal reserve would be

$$A_{y+t} \tag{7.12}$$

if the policy is paid-up at the first death, or

$$A_{y+t} - P \cdot \ddot{a}_{y+t} \tag{7.13}$$

if it is not.

Reserves for Frasier-Type Policies

For a Frasier-type policy, the reserve is independent of the first death status. Special functions must be calculated based on

$$\ell_{\overline{[x]+t:[y]+t}} = \ell_{\overline{xy}} \cdot (_tp_x + _tp_y - _tp_{xy}).$$

For a Frasier policy, the terminal reserve at duration t using the special functions is

$$A_{\overline{[x]+t:\overline{[y]+t}}} - P \cdot \ddot{a}_{\overline{[x]+t:\overline{[y]+t}}}. \tag{7.14}$$

Due to the special functions, $[x]+t:[y]+t$ is independent of whether one of either (x) or (y) has died. All that is known is that they were both alive at policy issue, and at least one is now alive.

Another issue with last-to-die (as well as first-to-die) policies of either type is the use of a joint equal age calculation. In order to simplify calculations (and allow the use of factor tapes), a joint equal age table is often used to find an age z, such that $A_{\overline{x+t:y+t}}$ may be replaced by $A_{\overline{z+t:z+t}}$ in the above calculations.[20]

Actuarial Guideline XX gives acceptable joint equal age rules for valuation of first-to-die products based on the 1980 CSO Table. Many companies use these rules for last-to-die policies, although the theoretical joint equal age treatment would be different for last-to-die policies, and many other rules are also in common use.

---

[20] Frequently, joint equal age tables are also used to translate the functions into one sex status to avoid the use of three sex combinations (male-male, male-female, female-female).

EXERCISES

1. A whole life policy issued in the U.S. has a gross premium of $8.60.

	Net Premium		$\ddot{a}_{x+t}$		$1000A_{x+t}$	
	4%	5.5%	4%	5.5%	4%	5.5%
80 CSO	12.89	10.16	17.00	14.42	346	248
58 CSO	14.22	11.40	16.36	13.98	371	271

What is the deficiency reserve under the 1976 amendments to the SVL at age $x + t$ (just before payment of the annual premium then due), in each of the following cases?

   (a) Both the policy's valuation basis and the minimum standard are 58 CSO 4%.
   (b) The policy's valuation basis is 58 CSO 4%, but the minimum standard is 58 CSO 5.5%.
   (c) The policy's valuation basis is 58 CSO 4%, but the minimum standard is 80 CSO 5.5%.

In each case, what is the total reserve required?

2. Compare and contrast U.S. and Canadian treatment of renewable term reserves.

3. Discuss considerations in setting lapse assumptions for Canadian term-to-100 policies.

4. Would the tenth year terminal reserve be larger for a Frasier-type or traditional last-to-die policy?

CHAPTER EIGHT

CASH FLOW TESTING

BACKGROUND

The earlier chapters in this book deal with the calculation methodologies and bases for several types of reserve factors that are required as part of a statutory valuation. The calculation of these factors is an important part of an actuary's work because the actuary is required to certify that the reserves meet minimum legal standards. Having done that, the important question remains to be answered: "Do the reserves make good and sufficient provision for the liabilities undertaken by the company?" Minimum valuation standards are generally intended to be conservative but are not always so. This can occur due to unexpected effects of product features, different marketing techniques, or as a result of simplifying procedures used in calculating statutory reserve factors.

As an example, consider the reserves for a single premium immediate annuity. The Standard Valuation Law will specify a maximum rate of interest that can be used in valuing these liabilities. For a given year's issues this interest is level forever. The interest rates in the Standard Valuation Law are currently dynamic and change with the investment environment. For example, the valuation interest rate for a single premium immediate annuity issued in 1982 was as high as 13.25%. Rates available on investments made during that period were well in excess of 13.25%. However, it is difficult to invest for the full benefit period associated with immediate annuities. Even if the company does invest fairly long, issuers of bonds may elect to call them if interest rates change. As a result, money might have to be reinvested at rates well below 13.25%.

In practice any number of events might occur that would make the statutory minimum reserves prescribed by law insufficient. The Standard Valuation Law cannot contemplate all of these items and therefore actuarial judgment and testing is required to ensure that reserves not only meet legal requirement but that the assets supporting the reserves are sufficient to cover outstanding liabilities.

Not too many years ago, a discussion of the good and sufficient provision would have emphasized gross premium valuations. A gross premium valuation involves the calculation of reserves, including best estimate assumptions and including all policyholder benefits and expenses. This sort of approach was suggested to cover the following situations:

(1) The statutory valuation methodology was deficient because it did not consider withdrawals or expenses.

(2) The experience mortality was actually higher than mortality contemplated by the statutory valuation standard.

(3) Reserve strengthening was needed due to investment yields not supporting the valuation interest rate.

Today this discussion leads to what has been termed the *valuation actuary* concept. The valuation actuary must consider whether or not reserves make good and sufficient provision for future obligations not only under expected experience but under a number of different scenarios that might be plausible.

The valuation actuary concept has led to the consideration of many different items that might affect the adequacy of reserves, including but not limited to the following:

(1) Cash flow testing that includes the interaction between assets and liabilities under a number of different interest scenarios.

(2) Estimating the impact of epidemics such as AIDS on the adequacy of the company's reserves.

(3) Evaluating the impact of mortality deterioration due to selective lapsation on certain types of term products.

The area currently receiving the most attention is cash flow testing. This chapter is devoted to that topic.

DEFINITION OF CASH FLOW TESTING

Cash flow testing has been defined by the Actuarial Standards Board as any projection of cash flows in which the specific timing of asset and liability cash flow is considered. The projection of these cash flows will involve many assumptions similar to those used in other more familiar types of actuarial projections. However, cash flow testing generally recognizes the following factors:

(1) The interrelationship between assumptions (i.e., between lapse rates and mortality rates, or between lapse rates and the difference between credited interest rates and competitor rates).[1]
(2) The interest rates or dividend rates offered by competitors.
(3) Investment yields available in the marketplace in general.
(4) Assumptions considering company policy with regard to non-guaranteed elements or dividends in different economic environments.

The types of assumptions generally required in performing cash flow testing designed specifically to measure interest rate risk are discussed later in this chapter, and an example is presented.

ASSUMPTIONS NEEDED

Future Economic Environments

To perform cash flow testing, the actuary must first choose a set of future economic scenarios under which the asset and liability cash flows will be calculated. There are several methods currently in use for selecting a set of scenarios. The pros and cons of the more common approaches currently in use will be discussed in this book.

---

[1] If a company's credited rates are noncompetitive, that company should experience higher lapses.

Handpicked Scenarios

Under this approach, scenarios are selected by choosing future interest rate scenarios that are of particular interest to the tester. This is the approach followed in both the regulations supporting the 1990 Standard Valuation Law, and in New York Regulation 126. The advantage of this approach, often referred to as a deterministic approach, is that the cash flow tester generally has more comfort with looking at results on a scenario-by-scenario basis, since he or she has constructed the scenarios. Scenarios constructed under this method tend to be easy to describe and can be generally categorized briefly as "rapidly increasing," "down and up," "wave," and so forth. The disadvantage of this approach is that it is very cumbersome to generate a large number of handpicked scenarios. Choosing handpicked scenarios can also lead to disagreement over the probability of a given scenario. In certain instances (reserve testing is probably one) a large set of scenarios may be necessary to generate statistical credibility. Finally, in practice handpicked scenarios tend to produce more favorable results than would be expected statistically.[2]

The Log-Normal Model

The *log-normal model* is discussed in academic research that has taken place over the past 20 years. This model was in use by non-actuaries who studied interest rate movements long before actuaries began performing cash flow testing.

Briefly the log-normal model is based on the following assumptions:
(1) The natural log of the ratio $\frac{i_{t+1}}{i_t}$ is a normal random variable, where i_t is a scenario interest rate.
(2) The mean is zero.
(3) The standard deviation is a measure of the volatility to be expected.

Using this model, different levels of standard deviation can be entered to reflect the volatility experienced over past periods of time.

---

[2] The tendency is to not pick severe scenarios, such as actually occurred between 1971 and 1991.

Generally, these parameters are used to generate a future short-term interest rate and a future long-term interest rate. Common rates used are 90-day rates and 10-year rates. Other rates are generally obtained through interpolation and functional relationships between the rates being projected and the rates of other securities.

Transition Probability Approach

Another approach is to define a universe of yield curves. This universe would contain many different interest rate levels and shapes of the yield curve. Once a set of standard yield curves has been developed a matrix of probabilities is defined with each probability representing the probability of a particular yield curve following the existing yield curve. Occasionally these probabilities are set by means of agreement between the actuaries and investment officers of the company performing the cash flow testing. After defining the universe of yield curves and the transition probabilities, current actual rates are examined and that yield curve is used as the starting yield curve. Monte Carlo simulation is then used to generate future yield curves for each succeeding period for as many periods into the future as required to define a scenario.

Competitor Rate or Market Rate Assumption

Many of the functional relationships in cash flow testing key off of the relationship between credited interest rates, market rates, and lapse rates. The *competitor rate* or *market rate* describes what is available to a policy-holder who lapses his policy and buys a comparable new policy. This market rate can be defined in terms of credited interest rates on a universal life policy or single premium deferred annuity policy or dividend rates on participating whole life policy.

The market rate is used to make an assessment of how competitive the policy is in a future scenario relative to the other options available to the policyholder. Obviously the company cannot sit down and do a competitive survey of financial products available in the future. As a simplifying assumption often the competitor rate is defined as a single interest rate. When defining the competitor rate it is important to consider your company's competitive profile and the characteristics of your policy (for example how important is the interest rate). If your product requires a credited rate in the top

10% of competitors to meet your competitive objectives, this should be reflected in your choice of a definition of competitor rate.

The graph on page 143 illustrates a competitor rate formula for a universal life policy designed to fit the median credited rate for existing universal life policies. The formula used ties back to past experience for the time period shown reasonably well for a product with an average credited rate.

Market rate assumptions will also depend on the type of product being studied. Often market rate assumptions are based on some function of a current interest rate and a moving average of an interest rate. The moving average is generally meant to reflect the impact of competitors who use portfolio rate crediting strategies, as well as a tendency for some companies to lag the market.

Nonguaranteed Elements Practices

For some contracts this is as simple as determining the interest rate crediting strategy. However, for others there is not a specific interest rate credit, but rather interest rates influence dividends or other non-guaranteed elements. In any event, the company must make some assumption regarding the impact of future economic environments on the benefits passed on to policyholders.

To keep our example simple, we will consider a Universal Life product that credits a company-declared rate. Some typical strategies include the following:

(1) Credit the earned rate less an investment margin.
(2) Credit some function of the market rate.
(3) Use a hybrid approach.

Other strategies might include multipliers rather than constant investment margins that would increase or decrease the investment margin as interest rates go up or down or as time passes.

Lapse Rates

The actuary must come up with a best estimate of future lapse rates and some decision about how lapses may depart from this best estimate if the economic environment changes. There is little experience with regard to the interaction

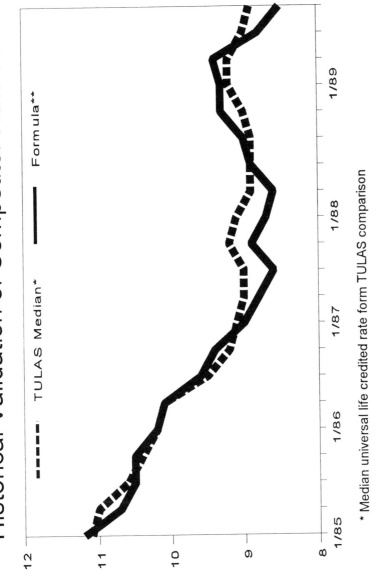

Historical Validation of Competitor Rate Form

- - - - TULAS Median*
——— Formula**

1/85 1/86 1/87 1/88 1/89

* Median universal life credited rate form TULAS comparison

** Competitor rate produced by the greater of:
- 87.5% of 2-quarter average of the 5-year scenario rate plus 1.31%
- 82.5% of 12-quarter average of the 5-year senario rate plus 1.25%

between lapse rates and credited rates on life insurance and annuities. There is some indication during the mid to late 1970s that as investment retures on alternate investments became very attractive, companies experienced higher than expected withdrawals of their cash values and extensive use of the policy loan provision. The lapse assumption is based upon the common sense argument that as policyholders' other options become more and more attractive they will be more likely to surrender their policies.

Items to consider in developing a lapse function include the following:

(1) The presence and level of any surrender charges. Many lapse rate functions take into account the level of surrender charge relative to policyholder account values.

(2) The marketing techniques and loyalty of the field force.

(3) The prominence of the interest rate in the marketing and maintenance of the policy. Arguments have been put forth that participating business may be less sensitive to excess lapses since the credited interest rate often is not obvious to the policyholder.

(4) Duration from issue.

(5) Type of products sold. Products that are pure investment products such as single premium deferred annuities might be more subject to excess lapsation than more protection-oriented products.

Tables 8.1 through 8.3, on pages 145-147, contain three examples of excess lapse formulas and the resulting excess lapses at various levels of surrender charges, market rates, and credited rates. Note that in all of these examples the excess lapses are a function of the competitor rate, the credited rate, and the surrender charge.

In practice, when performing cash flow testing the actuary must develop estimates of the amount of excess lapsation expected at different differentials between crediting rates and market rates, and adjust these for the expected impact of surrender charges. The parameters of the excess lapse formula would then be set to produce excess lapses of approximately this magnitude.

TABLE 8.1

EXCESS LAPSE RATES — I

Excess Lapse Rate:
$$\left[\left(\frac{M(100 \cdot D)^E}{100} \right)(1 - A \cdot S) - R \cdot S \right] \not< 0$$

Spread between the Competitor Rate and the Crediting Rate	··· Cash Value as a Percent of Fund ···				
	0%	25%	50%	75%	100%
1.00%	0.00%	0.00%	0.00%	0.00%	2.00%
1.25	0.00	0.00	0.00	1.41	3.91
1.50	0.00	0.00	1.75	4.25	6.75
1.75	0.72	3.22	5.72	8.22	10.72
2.00	6.00	8.50	11.00	13.50	16.00

FORMULA I:

Exponential Formula Parameters

Credited Rate Threshold:	0.0
Multiplier (M):	2.0
Exponent (E):	3.0
Additional Rate Ratio Multiplier (A):	0.0
Reduction to Additional Rate Multiplier (R):	0.1
Difference ($D > 0$):	

Competitor Rate − Current Credited Rate − Threshhold

SC Ratio (S): $1 - CSV/FUND$

TABLE 8.2

EXCESS LAPSE RATES — II

Excess Lapse Rate: $\left[\left(\frac{M(100\cdot D)^E}{100}\right)(1-A\cdot S)\ -\ R\cdot S\right]\ \not<\ 0$

Spread between the Competitor Rate and the Crediting Rate	··· Cash Value as a Percent of Fund ···				
	0%	25%	50%	75%	100%
1.00%	0.00%	0.50%	1.00%	1.50%	2.00%
1.25	0.00	0.98	1.95	2.93	3.91
1.50	0.00	1.69	3.38	5.06	6.75
1.75	0.00	2.68	5.36	8.04	10.72
2.00	0.00	4.00	8.00	12.00	16.00

FORMULA II:

Exponential Formula Parameters

Credited Rate Threshold:	0.0
Multiplier (M):	2.0
Exponent (E):	3.0
Additional Rate Ratio Multiplier (A):	1.0
Reduction to Additional Rate Multiplier (R):	0.0
Difference ($D > 0$):	

Competitor Rate — Current Credited Rate — Threshhold

SC Ratio (S): 1 — *CSV/FUND*

TABLE 8.3

EXCESS LAPSE RATES – III

Excess Lapse Rate:
$$\left[\left(\frac{M(100 \cdot D)^E}{100}\right)(1 - A \cdot S) - R \cdot S\right] \not< 0$$

Spread between the Competitor Rate and the Crediting Rate	··· Cash Value as a Percent of Fund ···				
	0%	25%	50%	75%	100%
1.00%	0.75%	0.94%	1.13%	1.31%	1.50%
1.25	1.05	1.31	1.57	1.83	2.10
1.50	1.38	1.72	2.07	2.41	2.76
1.75	1.72	2.17	2.60	3.04	3.47
2.00	2.12	2.65	3.18	3.71	4.24

FORMULA III:

Exponential Formula Parameters

Credited Rate Threshold:	0.0
Multiplier (M):	1.5
Exponent (E):	1.5
Additional Rate Ratio Multiplier (A):	0.5
Reduction to Additional Rate Multiplier (R):	0.0

Difference ($D > 0$):

Competitor Rate – Current Credited Rate – Threshhold

SC Ratio (S): $1 - CSV/FUND$

Reinvestment Strategies

In performing cash flow testing, the actuary and investment officer must work together to define how positive cash flows will be invested in the future. This is generally done either by specifying a portion of cash flows to be invested in each type of security or by maintaining a balance of each type of security in the total portfolio. As a simple example, a company might decide to invest 50% of each positive cash flow in ten-year Baa bonds and 50% in ten-year Treasuries. The second approach would be to maintain 50% of the total portfolio in each of these two securities and solve for the percentage of each cash flow that must be invested in each in order to maintain this balance. Obviously, real-life reinvestment strategies are more complicated.

The reinvestment strategy may also define situations under which it is anticipated that this strategy will change. Key examples of points in time that changes in reinvestment strategies might be projected to occur include inversions of yield curves, increases or decreases in interest rates above specified levels, or durational-based changes in reinvestment strategy.

In setting up the parameters for cash flow study, a decision must also be made with regard to negative cash flows. If negative cash flows occur in the projection, they may be modeled by selling assets, by buying negative assets (this is used to simulate borrowing between lines of business, and has a similar impact to selling assets), or borrowing at a short-term rate.

CASE STUDY

A company sold a single Universal Life plan from 1985 to 1989. At December 31, 1989, the company calculated statutory reserves of 57,279,664 using a static valuation method. The valuation actuary has been asked to consider whether these reserves make good and sufficient provision for outstanding obligations under a variety of future economic conditions. The actuary decides to perform cash flow testing using some of the techniques described in this chapter. The assumptions are described in Appendix E.

After checking with the investment department, the actuary finds that the assets are invested in Baa bonds with maturities ranging from 1994 to 2004 (5 to 15 years).

The investment department intends to reinvest positive cash flows 50% in 10-year Baa bonds and 50% in 20-year Baa bonds. Working with the marketing and investment departments, the actuary determines the crediting strategy to be that described in Appendix E; the company will attempt to stay close to its competitors. They therefore expect to occasionally sacrifice investment margins and avoid excess lapsation. The actuary has told the interest-crediting committee that an alternative strategy that occasionally falls well behind the competition and produces excess lapse potential could be as profitable. The committee decides not to explore this strategy because they feel market image would suffer.

The actuary then projects both the assets and Universal Life product cash flows under 200 future interest rate scenarios. To see if 200 scenarios will yield a better indication of the range of possible results than a smaller number of scenarios, the actuary generates five separate sets of 40 scenarios.

For each scenario, the actuary calculates a variety of financial measures, including the present value of statutory profits and the surplus at the end of the projection.

Using the first measure and a discount rate that is based on the interest rate scenario, the actuary estimates the extra reserve necessary to eliminate negatives in all scenarios and the extra reserve necessary to eliminate negatives in at least 90% of the scenarios. The results are shown in the following table.

TABLE 8.4

EXTRA RESERVE REQUIRED
(in thousands)

Scenario Set	Confidence Level 100%	90%
1	10,808	475
2	11,511	7,233
3	22,260	5,015
4	15,582	670
5	5,698	1,495
All	22,260	3,348

Table 8.4 shows that a cash flow study based on 40 scenarios would produce a potentially incomplete estimate of the range of possible results.

The actuary also examined the mean present value of statutory profits from each scenario set. The results are shown in Table 8.5 on the following page.

TABLE 8.5

MEAN PRESENT VALUE OF PROFITS
(in thousands)

Scenario Set	Scenario Rate	15%
1	20,939	12,352
2	18,187	11,402
3	17,187	10,156
4	18,958	11,464
5	20,408	12,229
All	19,136	11,521

The actuary prepares a report for management showing the change in the value of inforce business and the estimated value of new business. After reviewing the above results, the actuary feels that 40 scenarios may be sufficient to estimate the expected value of new sales.

Sensitivity Tests

Upon reviewing the results of this cash flow testing, the president was alarmed by two concerns: the amount of additional reserves required, and the seemingly large variation in the value of future profits. The actuary was asked to review the assumptions.

The actuary confessed that there is little available data upon to which base excess lapse assumptions. However, it was noted that the crediting strategy to which the company president is firmly committed does not result in significant excess lapses. The actuary also admitted that predicting competitors' rates into the future can be difficult and offered to perform a sensitivity test on the competitor rate assumption. Noting the close fit between the actuary's competitor rate assumption and historical experience, the company president chose not to pursue this avenue.

In the meeting with the president, the investment department, and the actuarial department, it was suggested that alternate investment strategies be reviewed that might produce less risk to the company. The investment department wanted to experiment with mortgage-backed securities and the actuaries wanted to shorten the period to maturity. An alternate reinvestment "strategy" was chosen. For Strategy B, 50% of the book value of assets was maintained in ten-year GNMAE's and 50% was maintained in five-year Baa bonds.

Using this strategy, the average present value of statutory profits at 15% actually improved and the standard deviation was reduced dramatically. The results are shown in the following table.

TABLE 8.6

INVESTMENT STRATEGY B

Scenario Set	Standard Mean (in thousands)	Deviation (in thousands)
1	16,911	1,881
2	17,646	4,702
3	16,097	2,468
4	16,689	2,162
5	16,873	1,801

The corresponding standard deviations for the original strategy were much higher, generally in the 6 million to 7.5 million range.

In fact, after reviewing the results under Investment Strategy B, the actuary felt that if the investment department were to immediately trade the existing assets and follow this investment strategy forward, then the existing level of statutory reserves should be adequate.

EXERCISES

1. Discuss the advantages and disadvantages of alternative approaches to selecting economic scenarios.

2. Why will the choice of the appropriate lapse function used in cash flow testing always require actuarial judgment?

3. Discuss the extra assumptions needed for cash flow testing that are not required when performing a traditional U.S. statutory valuation.

CHAPTER NINE

THE VALUATION ACTUARY

The NAIC model Standard Valuation Law was amended in December 1990 to incorporate the valuation actuary concept. Under these amendments, every U.S. life company, unless exempted,[1] must submit an actuarial opinion that considers not only the liabilities, but the ability of the cash flows of the assets to make sufficient provision for the liabilities of the company. The 1990 revisions are based on the earlier New York Regulation 126, which is paralleled in many ways by the new law.

The Actuarial Standards Board (ASB) has also issued Actuarial Standards of Practice (ASP) 7 and 14. ASP 7 gives guidance to actuaries on how to perform cash flow testing. ASP 14 provides guidance on when to perform cash flow testing. In reviewing these actuarial standards of practice, readers must be aware of the ASB's approach to setting standards. This approach is probably best characterized by statements made by Harold G. Ingraham, Jr., former president of the Society of Actuaries, at the April 30 - May 1, 1990 meeting of the Society:

"The ASB also has made it plain that it won't permit the setting of rigid standards. Its members believe that standards of practice must be conceptualized and worded in such a way that they don't unnecessarily circumscribe an actuary's creativity in approaching new problems. In other words, the ASB endorses what it refers to as the 'disclosed defendable deviation' approach. And the ASB has specifi-

---

[1] Certain companies meeting size and mix of business requirements are exempted.

cally instructed its operating committees 'to avoid being overly pre-scriptive and to allow the actuary to deviate when he or she has justi-fication.'"

The following provides a brief overview of the provisions of the model Stand-ard Valuation Law amendments, the associated model regulation, and the actuarial standards of practice as they relate to the 1990 SVL.

PROVISIONS OF MODEL
STANDARD VALUATION LAW

Opinion of Appointed Actuary

The *appointed actuary* must submit a Statement of Actuarial Opinion as to whether the reserves and related actuarial items are computed appropriately, are based on assumptions which satisfy contractual provisions, are consistent with prior reported amounts, and comply with applicable laws of the state. The opinion applies to all business in force including individual and group plans and is subject to standards adopted from time to time by the ASB. The commissioner may, by regulation, prescribe other standards.

Qualifications and Professional Liability

For purposes of the model Standard Valuation Law, an appointed actuary is a qualified actuary who is appointed or retained by the board of directors of the company to prepare the Statement of Actuarial Opinion. A qualified actuary is a member in good standing of the American Academy of Actuaries, who is qualified to sign statements of actuarial opinion for life and health insurance companies in accordance with the Academy's qualification standards, and who also meets certain requirements set forth by the commissioner.

Other than in cases of fraud or willful misconduct, the appointed actuary, according to the model Standard Valuation Law, shall not be liable for damages to any person other than the insurance company and the commis-sioner for any act, error, omission, decision, or conduct, with respect to the actuary's opinion. The model Standard Valuation Law thus attempts to exempt the actuary from "third party liability."

The model Standard Valuation Law is being adopted with some variations on a state-by-state basis. For example, in some states the actuary is not specifically exempted from third party liability.

Supporting Memorandum

In accordance with a model regulation supplementing the new Standard Valuation Law, an actuarial memorandum must be prepared which is supportive of the actuarial opinion. If the company fails to provide a supporting memorandum, the commissioner may engage a qualified actuary at the expense of the company. The supporting memorandum is a confidential document according to the model Standard Valuation Law.

Transition Period for Higher Reserves

The model law provides for a transition period for any additional reserves that the actuary may decide are required.

Required Analysis

The model regulation requires that a certain minimum amount of analysis be performed. This analysis includes cash flow testing under seven prescribed scenarios that are similar to those used in New York Regulation 126. These interest scenarios are described in the following table.

Scenario	Description
1	Level
2	Uniformly increasing 5% over 10 years and then level
3	Uniformly increasing 5% over 5 years, then uniformly decreasing 5% over next 5 years and then level
4	A 3% pop-up and then level
5	Uniformly decreasing 5% over 10 years and then level
6	Uniformly decreasing 5% over 5 years, then uniformly increasing 5% over next 5 years and then level
7	A 3% pop-down and then level

All rates in the preceding scenarios are subject to a 4% minimum and a 25% maximum.

The model regulation indicates that beginning interest rates may be based on interest rates close to the valuation date on new investments that are comparable to those being purchased to support the product liabilities being tested, or may be based on an outside index, such as Treasury yields, of assets of the appropriate length on a date close to the valuation date.

Additional Analysis

In addition to the seven required scenarios, additional analysis may be deemed necessary by the valuation actuary. For example, one actuarial consulting firm added Scenarios 8, 9, and 10 for 1992, which are the same as Scenarios 5, 6, and 7, except that rates are subject to a minimum of 2.5% instead of 4%. Short-term U.S. Treasury rates at the time were close to 4%, and it appeared likely that these rates, as well as certain longer term rates, could pierce the 4% minimum. The 2.5% minimum was arbitrarily selected to test the effect of rates dropping further.

Lastly, the same firm included a Scenario 11 which was similar to Scenario 3, except that it contained an inversion of the yield curve.

The tests should cover as many alternative interest rate scenarios as the valuation actuary deems necessary to generate an understanding of the dynamics relating the insurance and investment cash flows. In line with this objective, consideration should be given to supplemental testing based on a set of stochastic interest rate scenarios.

Considerations

In developing the required set of seven interest rate scenarios, consideration must be given to the following items:

(1) The point in time or period over which the starting rates are based.

(2) The shape of the ultimate yield curve.

(3) The application of the minimum rate constraint.

With respect to the first item, the model regulation indicates that starting rates should be based on applicable investment yields close to the valuation date. For Treasury yields, reasonable interpretations of this guidance might include (a) the rate on the last reported day closest to the valuation date, (b) the average of rates for the last full week closest to the valuation date, or (c) the average of rates for the last full month closest to the valuation date. Referring to Regulation 126, the New York Insurance Department has indicated a preference for using the last reported day closest to the valuation date.

With respect to the second item, a decision must be made either to maintain the shape of the starting yield curve in all future years or to assume that a more "normal" shape of the yield curve ultimately applies. Under Regulation 126, the New York Insurance Department has indicated that either approach is acceptable regarding the shape of the ultimate yield curve.

Maintaining the shape of the starting yield curve might be supported by the following reasoning:

(1) The selection of the shape of the ultimate yield curve would be somewhat arbitrary.

(2) The shape of the yield curve may be dependent on the level of rates which would suggest selecting not one but a multitude of curves.

(3) The desire for simplicity.

With respect to the third item, it would seem to make sense to apply the minimum rate constraint to each rate after first having determined what the rates would be without such minimum.

Under each of the seven scenarios, and as many other as the actuary deems necessary to form an opinion, the actuary must examine the cash flow characteristics of the business. This analysis involves the development of assumptions regarding policyholder and corporate behavior described in Chapter 8.

There are currently no regulatory or professional standards which identify precisely the number of scenarios that should be tested nor the number of scenarios that a company must pass in order that reserves are deemed adequate.

ACTUARIAL STANDARD OF PRACTICE NO. 7

In July 1991, the Actuarial Standards Board adopted ASP 7, which identifies recommended practices and considerations regarding cash flow analysis. This standard of practice provides general guidance on how to perform cash flow analysis. Some notable examples include the following:

(1) With regard to scenarios, ASP 7 requires that the actuary be satisfied that the scenarios tested reflect a range of conditions that are consistent with the pur-pose of the cash flow test.

(2) In determining the number of scenarios, the actuary should choose a number that will reflect the range of conditions that is consistent with the purpose of the cash flow test. The actuary should also consider the relative importance of different risks and should also disclose any limitations of the analysis due to the number, types, or likelihood of scenarios tested.

(3) The actuary should consider the sensitivity of the model to the effect of variations in key assumptions and the actuary should be satisfied that sensitivity testing has been adequately addressed.

(4) The actuarial standard of practice also provides general guidance on items to consider in projecting both asset and liability cash flows.

ASP 7 provides general guidance on "items that should be considered when performing cash flow analysis rather than specific examples of how to perform cash flow analysis for specific types of questions."

ACTUARIAL STANDARD OF PRACTICE NO. 14

ASP 14 deals with when to perform cash flow testing for life and health insurance companies. Its purpose is to give guidance to the actuary in determining whether or not to perform cash flow testing as part of forming a professional opinion or recommendation. The scope applies to all work performed by the actuary for a life or health insurance company. Areas of actuarial analysis where cash flow testing might be appropriate, according to standards, include the following:

(1) Product design and pricing studies.

(2) Evaluation of investment strategies.

(3) Testing the policyholder dividend scales and future non-guaranteed elements.

(4) Long-term financial projections and forecasts.

(5) Reserve testing.

(6) Actuarial appraisals of insurance companies or blocks of business.

ASP 14 requires the actuary to exercise considerable judgment in determining whether or not cash flow testing is required. The items the actuary should consider in making this judgment include the following:

(1) The sensitivity of liability cash flows to changing investment environments.
(2) The composition of assets supporting reserves. (Do they contain liberal call provisions or prepayment options?)
(3) Any significant reinvestment risk to which the liabilities expose the company.

ASP 14 makes it clear that cash flow testing is not always necessary. However, it is up to the actuary to make that judgement. ASP 14 does provide some examples of situations where cash flow testing may not be necessary, including the following:

(1) Short-term products.
(2) Products where the cash flows are relatively insensitive to changes in economic conditions.
(3) Situations where the valuation actuary can demonstrate that experience will almost certainly be less severe than provided for in the reserves.
(4) Situations where prior cash flow analysis has shown the results to be relatively insensitive to economic changes.

The need for cash flow analysis should be considered in almost every aspect of the actuary's work. If, however, the actuary feels sufficiently confident that the results will not be sensitive to such analysis, the analysis need not be performed. Often it would be difficult to make such a statement without first performing at least a limited analysis.

APPENDIX A

Prevailing State Assumed Interest Rates
and
Prevailing Commissioners' Standard Tables[1]

Life Insurance and Supplementary Total
and Permanent Disability Benefits

| | | Tables[3] | | |
| | | Ordinary Contracts | | |
Issue Year	Interest Rate[2]	Life	Disability	Industrial Policies
1948-60	3.5%	CSO 41	C3DT 26	SI 41
1961-62	3.5	CSO 58(a)	C3DT 26	SI 41
1963	3.5	CSO 58(a)	P2DS 52	SI 41
1964-74	3.5	CSO 58(a)	P2DS 52	CSI 61
1975-79	4.0	CSO 58(a)	P2DS 52	CSI 61
1980-82	4.5	CSO 58(b)	P2DS 52	CSI 61
1983-85	6.0[4]	CSO 80	P2DS 52	CSI 61
1986	6.0[4]	CSO 80(b)	P2DS 52	CSI 61
1987-92	5.5[4]	CSO 80(b)	P2DS 52	CSI 61
1993-94	5.0[4]	CSO 80(b)	P2DS 52	CSI 61
1995-96	4.5[4]	CSO 80(b)	P2DS 52	CSI 61

See pages 163-164 for explanatory notes.

Prevailing State Assumed Interest Rates
and
Prevailing Commissioners' Standard Tables[1]

	Individual Annuities and Pure Endowments			
	Interest Rates			
Issue Year	Immediate	S.P. Deferred	All Other	Tables[3]
1948-62	3.5%	3.5%	3.5%	SA 37
1963-74	3.5	3.5	3.5	A 49
1975-79	6.0	4.0	4.0	IA 71
1980-82	7.5	5.5	4.5	IA 71
1983-84	1980[4]	1980[4]	1980[4]	IA 71
1985-95	1980[4]	1980[4]	1980[4]	IA 83

	Group Annuities and Pure Endowments	
Issue Year	Interest Rates	Tables[3]
1948-62	3.5%	SA 37
1963-74	3.5	GA 51
1975-79	6.0	GA 71
1980-82	7.5	GA 71
1983-84	1980[4]	GA 71
1985-95	1980[4]	GA 83

See pages 163-164 for explanatory notes.

Notes to Appendix A

1. Highest interest rate and most recent mortality table permitted as of January 1 of the stated year, for valuation of contracts of the specified type issued in that year, under the valuation laws of at least 26 states. Prior to 1946 the prevailing interest rate was 4%; in 1946 and 1947 it was 3.5%.

2. Interest rates for all life insurance, including ordinary, industrial, group and credit.

3. CSO 41:   Commissioners 1941 Standard Ordinary Mortality Table
   CSO 58:   Commissioners 1958 Standard Ordinary Mortality Table
       (a) For issues of 1961 through 1979, female mortality rates under the CSO 58 Table are equal to those for males 3 years younger, with sex-distinct rates for ages below 15.
       (b) For issue years after 1979, female mortality rates under the CSO 58 Table are equal to those for males 6 year younger, with sex-distinct rates for ages below 20.
   CSO 80:   Commissioners 1980 Standard Ordinary Mortality Table
       (a) The CSO 80 Table is a sex-distinct table which can be used for statutory valuations with or without select mortality factors.
       (b) As of 1986, the CSO 80 smoker/nonsmoker distinct tables were approved in 26 states. These tables may be optionally used, in lieu of the original CSO 80 table, on a plan-by-plan basis.
   C3DT 26:   Class (3) 1926 Disability Table
   P2DS 52:   The tables of Period 2 disablement rates and the 1930 to 1950 termination rates of the 1952 Disability Study of the Society of Actuaries.
   SI 41:   1941 Standard Industrial Mortality Table
   CSI 61:   Commissioners 1961 Standard Industrial Mortality Table
   SA 37:   Standard Annuity Mortality Table
   A 49:   Annuity Mortality Table for 1949 (Ultimate)
   IA 71:   1971 Individual Annuity Mortality Table
   IA 83:   1983 Individual Annuity Mortality Table (Table a)
   GA 51:   Group Annuity Mortality Table for 1951

GA 71: 1971 Group Annuity Mortality Table
GA 83: 1983 Group Annuity Mortality Table

4. Under the 1980 amendments to the Standard Valuation Law, interest rates vary by product feature and according to a prescribed index. The rate illustrated for life insurance is that used for products of more than 20 years duration. Rates for other life and annuity products are illustrated in Appendix B.

APPENDIX B

Statutory Calendar Year Interest Rates
Based on NAIC Standard Valuation Laws

LIFE INSURANCE

		Guaranteed Duration	
Year	10 Years or Less	10+ to 20 Years	More Than 20 Years
1982	6.75%	6.25%	5.50%
1983-86	7.25	6.75	6.00
1987	6.50	6.00	5.50
1988-92	6.00	6.00	5.50
1993	6.00	6.00	5.00
1994	5.50	5.25	5.00
1995-6	5.50	5.25	4.50

SINGLE PREMIUM IMMEDIATE ANNUITIES

(Including annuity benefits involving life contingencies arising from other annuities with cash settlement options, and from guaranteed interest contracts with cash settlement options)

Year	Valuation Interest Rate	Year	Valuation Interest Rate
1981	11.50%	1989	8.75%
1982	13.25	1990	8.25
1983	11.25	1991	8.25
1984	11.25	1992	7.75
1985	11.00	1993	7.00
1986	9.25	1994	6.50
1987	8.00	1995	7.25
1988	8.75		

OTHER ANNUITIES AND
GUARANTEED INTEREST CONTRACTS

Cash Settlement Options?	Future Interest Guarantee?	Guarantee Duration (Years)	Formula Calendar (Year)	Valuation Interest Rate For Plan Type		
				A	B	C

Contracts Valued on an Issue Year Basis:

Cash Settlement Options?	Future Interest Guarantee?	Guarantee Duration (Years)	Formula Calendar (Year)	A	B	C
Yes	Yes	5 or Less	81	11.50%	9.50%	8.25%
			82	13.25	10.50	9.25
			83	11.25	9.25	8.25
			84	11.25	9.25	8.00
			85	11.00	9.00	8.00
			86	9.25	7.75	6.75
			87	8.00	6.75	6.25
			88	8.75	7.50	6.75
			89	8.75	7.25	6.50
			90	8.25	7.00	6.25
			91	8.25	7.00	6.25
			92	7.75	6.50	6.00
			93	7.00	6.00	5.50
			94	6.50	5.75	5.25
			95	7.25	6.25	5.75
Yes	Yes	more than 5 but not more than 10	81	11.00%	9.50%	8.25%
			82	12.50	10.50	9.25
			83	10.75	9.25	8.25
			84	10.75	9.25	8.00
			85	10.50	9.00	8.00
			86	8.75	7.75	6.75
			87	7.75	6.75	6.25
			88	8.50	7.50	6.75
			89	8.25	7.25	6.50
			90	8.00	7.00	6.25
			91	8.00	7.00	6.25
			92	7.50	6.50	6.00
			93	6.75	6.00	5.50
			94	6.50	5.75	5.25
			95	7.00	6.25	5.75

OTHER ANNUITIES AND
GUARANTEED INTEREST CONTRACTS

Cash Settlement Options?	Future Interest Guarantee?	Guarantee Duration (Years)	Formula Calendar (Year)	Valuation Interest Rate For Plan Type		
				A	B	C

Contracts Valued on an Issue Year Basis:

Cash Settlement Options?	Future Interest Guarantee?	Guarantee Duration (Years)	Formula Calendar (Year)	A	B	C
Yes	Yes	more than 10 but not more than 20	81	7.75%	6.75%	6.25%
			82	8.50	7.25	6.75
			83	8.25	7.00	6.75
			84	8.25	7.00	6.75
			85	8.25	7.00	6.50
			86	7.50	6.50	6.00
			87	7.00	6.00	5.75
			88	7.25	6.25	6.00
			89	7.25	6.25	6.00
			90	7.00	6.25	5.75
			91	7.00	6.25	5.75
			92	6.75	6.00	5.75
			93	6.25	5.50	5.25
			94	6.00	5.25	5.00
			95	6.25	5.50	5.25
Yes	Yes	more than 20	81	6.25%	5.50%	5.50%
			82	6.75	6.00	6.00
			83	6.75	5.75	5.75
			84	6.75	5.75	5.75
			85	6.50	5.75	5.75
			86	6.00	5.50	5.50
			87	5.75	5.25	5.25
			88	6.00	5.25	5.25
			89	6.00	5.25	5.25
			90	5.75	5.25	5.25
			91	5.75	5.25	5.25
			92	5.75	5.00	5.00
			93	5.25	4.75	4.75
			94	5.00	4.50	4.50
			95	5.25	4.75	4.75

OTHER ANNUITIES AND
GUARANTEED INTEREST CONTRACTS

Cash Settlement Options?	Future Interest Guarantee?	Guarantee Duration (Years)	Formula Calendar (Year)	Valuation Interest Rate For Plan Type		
				A	B	C

Contracts Valued on an Issue Year Basis:

Cash Settlement Options?	Future Interest Guarantee?	Guarantee Duration (Years)	Formula Calendar (Year)	A	B	C
Yes	No	5 or Less	81	12.00%	10.00%	9.00%
			82	13.75	11.25	10.00
			83	11.75	9.75	8.75
			84	11.75	9.75	8.50
			85	11.50	9.50	8.50
			86	9.50	8.00	7.25
			87	8.50	7.25	6.50
			88	9.25	7.75	7.00
			89	9.00	7.50	7.00
			90	8.50	7.25	6.50
			91	8.75	7.25	6.75
			92	8.00	6.75	6.25
			93	7.25	6.25	5.75
			94	6.75	6.00	5.50
			95	7.50	6.50	6.00
Yes	No	more than 5 but not more than 10	81	11.50%	10.00%	9.00%
			82	13.25	11.25	10.00
			83	11.25	9.75	8.75
			84	11.25	9.75	8.50
			85	11.00	9.50	8.50
			86	9.25	8.00	7.25
			87	8.00	7.25	6.50
			88	8.75	7.75	7.00
			89	8.75	7.50	7.00
			90	8.25	7.25	6.50
			91	8.25	7.25	6.75
			92	7.75	6.75	6.25
			93	7.00	6.25	5.75
			94	6.50	6.00	5.50
			95	7.25	6.50	6.00

OTHER ANNUITIES AND
GUARANTEED INTEREST CONTRACTS

Cash Settlement Options?	Future Interest Guarantee?	Guarantee Duration (Years)	Formula Calendar (Year)	Valuation Interest Rate For Plan Type A	B	C

Contracts Valued on an Issue Year Basis:

Cash Settlement Options?	Future Interest Guarantee?	Guarantee Duration (Years)	Formula Calendar (Year)	A	B	C
Yes	No	more than 10 but not more than 20	81	8.00%	7.00%	6.75%
			82	8.75	7.50	7.25
			83	8.75	7.50	7.00
			84	8.75	7.50	7.00
			85	8.50	7.50	7.00
			86	7.75	6.75	6.50
			87	7.25	6.50	6.00
			88	7.50	6.50	6.25
			89	7.50	6.50	6.25
			90	7.50	6.50	6.25
			91	7.50	6.50	6.25
			92	7.00	6.25	6.00
			93	6.50	5.75	5.50
			94	6.25	5.50	5.25
			95	6.50	5.75	5.50
Yes	No	more than 20	81	6.75%	6.00%	6.00%
			82	7.25	6.25	6.25
			83	7.00	6.25	6.25
			84	7.00	6.25	6.25
			85	7.00	6.25	6.25
			86	6.50	5.75	5.75
			87	6.00	5.50	5.50
			88	6.25	5.75	5.75
			89	6.25	5.50	5.50
			90	6.25	5.50	5.50
			91	6.25	5.50	5.50
			92	6.00	5.25	5.25
			93	5.50	5.00	5.00
			94	5.25	4.75	4.75
			95	5.50	5.00	5.00

OTHER ANNUITIES AND
GUARANTEED INTEREST CONTRACTS

Cash Settlement Options?	Future Interest Guarantee?	Guarantee Duration (Years)	Formula Calendar (Year)	Valuation Interest Rate For Plan Type		
				A	B	C

Contracts Valued on an Issue Year Basis:

No	Yes or No	10 or less		Same as with cash settlement and future interest guarantee for Plan Type A		
No	Yes or No	more than 10 but not more than 20	81	10.00%	Not applicable for any guarantee duration for Plan Types B and C	
			82	11.25		
			83	9.75		
			84	7.50		
			85	9.50		
			86	8.00		
			87	7.25		
			88	7.75		
			89	7.50		
			90	7.25		
			91	7.25		
			92	6.75		
			93	6.25		
			94	6.00		
			95	6.50		
No	Yes or No	more than 20	81	7.75%	Not applicable for any guarantee duration for Plan Types B and C	
			82	8.75		
			83	7.75		
			84	7.50		
			85	7.50		
			86	6.50		
			87	6.00		
			88	6.25		
			89	6.25		
			90	6.00		
			91	6.00		
			92	5.75		
			93	5.25		
			94	5.00		
			95	5.50		

OTHER ANNUITIES AND
GUARANTEED INTEREST CONTRACTS

Cash Settlement Options?	Future Interest Guarantee?	Guarantee Duration (Years)	Formula Calendar (Year)	Valuation Interest Rate For Plan Type		
				A	B	C

Contracts Valued on a Change-in-Fund Basis:

Cash Settlement Options?	Future Interest Guarantee?	Guarantee Duration (Years)	Formula Calendar (Year)	A	B	C
Yes	Yes	5 or less	81	13.25%	12.00%	9.00%
			82	15.00	13.75	10.00
			83	12.75	11.75	8.75
			84	12.75	11.75	8.50
			85	12.50	11.50	8.50
			86	10.25	9.50	7.25
			87	9.00	8.50	6.50
			88	10.00	9.25	7.00
			89	9.75	9.00	7.00
			90	9.25	8.50	6.50
			91	9.25	8.75	6.75
			92	8.50	8.00	6.25
			93	7.75	7.25	5.75
			94	7.25	6.75	5.50
			95	8.25	7.50	6.00
Yes	Yes	more than 5 but not more than 10	81	12.75%	12.00%	9.00%
			82	14.50	13.75	10.00
			83	12.25	11.75	8.75
			84	12.25	11.75	8.50
			85	12.00	11.50	8.50
			86	10.00	9.50	7.25
			87	8.75	8.50	6.50
			88	9.50	9.25	7.00
			89	9.50	9.00	7.00
			90	8.75	8.50	6.50
			91	9.00	8.75	6.75
			92	8.25	8.00	6.25
			93	7.50	7.25	5.75
			94	7.00	6.75	5.50
			95	8.00	7.50	6.00

OTHER ANNUITIES AND
GUARANTEED INTEREST CONTRACTS

Cash Settlement Options?	Future Interest Guarantee?	Guarantee Duration (Years)	Formula Calendar (Year)	Valuation Interest Rate For Plan Type A	B	C
Contracts Valued on a Change-in-Fund Basis:						
Yes	Yes	more than 10	81	11.50%	11.00%	8.25%
		but not more	82	13.25	12.50	9.25
		than 20	83	11.25	10.75	8.25
			84	11.25	10.75	8.00
			85	11.00	10.50	8.00
			86	9.25	8.75	6.75
			87	8.00	7.75	6.25
			88	8.75	8.50	6.75
			89	8.75	8.25	6.50
			90	8.25	8.00	6.25
			91	8.25	8.00	6.25
			92	7.75	7.50	6.00
			93	7.00	6.75	5.50
			94	6.50	6.50	5.25
			95	7.25	7.00	5.75
Yes	Yes	more than 20	81	9.50%	9.50%	7.25%
			82	10.50	10.50	8.00
			83	9.25	9.25	7.25
			84	9.25	9.25	7.25
			85	9.00	9.00	7.00
			86	7.75	7.75	6.00
			87	6.75	6.75	5.50
			88	7.50	7.50	6.00
			89	7.25	7.25	5.75
			90	7.00	7.00	5.50
			91	7.00	7.00	5.75
			92	6.50	6.50	5.25
			93	6.00	6.00	5.00
			94	5.75	5.75	4.75
			95	6.25	6.25	5.25

OTHER ANNUITIES AND
GUARANTEED INTEREST CONTRACTS

Cash Settlement Options?	Future Interest Guarantee?	Guarantee Duration (Years)	Formula Calendar (Year)	Valuation Interest Rate For Plan Type A	B	C

Contracts Valued on a Change-in-Fund Basis:

Cash Settlement Options?	Future Interest Guarantee?	Guarantee Duration (Years)	Formula Calendar (Year)	A	B	C
Yes	No	5 or less	81	13.75%	12.75%	9.50%
			82	15.75	14.50	10.50
			83	13.50	12.25	9.25
			84	13.25	12.25	9.25
			85	13.00	12.00	9.00
			86	10.75	10.00	7.75
			87	9.50	8.75	6.75
			88	10.25	9.50	7.50
			89	10.00	9.50	7.25
			90	9.50	8.75	7.00
			91	9.75	9.00	7.00
			92	9.00	8.25	6.50
			93	8.25	7.50	6.00
			94	7.50	7.00	5.75
			95	8.50	8.00	6.25
Yes	No	more than 5 but not more than 10	81	13.25%	12.75%	9.50%
			82	15.00	14.50	10.50
			83	12.75	12.25	9.25
			84	12.75	12.25	9.25
			85	12.50	12.00	9.00
			86	10.25	10.00	7.75
			87	9.00	8.75	6.75
			88	10.00	9.50	7.50
			89	9.75	9.50	7.25
			90	9.25	8.75	7.00
			91	9.25	9.00	7.00
			92	8.50	8.25	6.50
			93	7.75	7.50	6.00
			94	7.25	7.00	5.75
			95	8.25	8.00	6.25

OTHER ANNUITIES AND
GUARANTEED INTEREST CONTRACTS

Cash Settlement Options?	Future Interest Guarantee?	Guarantee Duration (Years)	Formula Calendar (Year)	Valuation Interest Rate For Plan Type		
				A	B	C

Contracts Valued on a Change-in-Fund Basis

Cash Settlement Options?	Future Interest Guarantee?	Guarantee Duration (Years)	Formula Calendar (Year)	A	B	C
Yes	No	more than 10 but not more than 20	81	12.00%	11.50%	9.00%
			82	13.75	13.25	10.00
			83	11.75	11.25	8.75
			84	11.75	11.25	8.50
			85	11.50	11.00	8.50
			86	9.50	9.25	7.25
			87	8.50	8.00	6.50
			88	9.25	8.75	7.00
			89	9.00	8.75	7.00
			90	8.50	8.25	6.50
			91	8.75	8.25	6.75
			92	8.00	7.75	6.25
			93	7.25	7.00	5.75
			94	6.75	6.50	5.50
			95	7.50	7.25	6.00
Yes	No	more than 20	81	10.00%	10.00%	7.75%
			82	11.25	11.25	8.75
			83	9.75	9.75	7.75
			84	9.75	9.75	7.50
			85	9.50	9.50	7.50
			86	8.00	8.00	6.50
			87	7.25	7.25	6.00
			88	7.75	7.75	6.25
			89	7.50	7.50	6.25
			90	7.25	7.25	6.00
			91	7.25	7.25	6.00
			92	6.75	6.75	5.75
			93	6.25	6.25	5.25
			94	6.00	6.00	5.00
			95	6.50	6.50	5.50

APPENDIX C

Product Used for Examples in Chapter 4

Endowment at 95
Valuation basis: 4.5% 58 CSO
Guaranteed COI based on 58 CSO ANB
Current COI equals guaranteed COI
Male, age 35, level total death benefit
Death benefit corridor equal to TRA 84 250% corridor

Example	Loads Front-End	Loads Back-End	Interest Guarantee
A	3% of Premiums	125% of Target Premium; grades to zero in year 16	4.0%
B	3% of Premiums	Same as A	4.0
C	None	Same as A	4.5
D	3% of Premiums	Same as A	4.5

Calculations of Present Value of Future Benefits
for Example A

The following values are given:

$$GMP = 14.49 \qquad GMF_{10} = 136.70 \qquad Fund_{10} = 195.75$$

From these values we find future guaranteed death benefits as follows:

Duration	Average Death Benefit	Duration	Average Death Benefit
11-36	1000	51	1753
37	1005	52	1823
38	1033	53	1893
39	1064	54	1965
40	1096	55	2037
41	1129	56	2110
42	1185	57	2165
43	1242	58	2224
44	1301	59	2290
45	1361	60	2360
46	1423	Endowment	2384.81
47	1486	at 95	
48	1551		
49	1617		
50	1684		

The present value of the above benefits, at the end of duration 10, is 381.65, based on 4.5% 1958 CSO continuous functions.

APPENDIX D

Reserves for Fixed Premium Universal Life

The following demonstration shows that surrender charges may be chosen such that the CRVM reserve for a fixed premium Universal Life policy will always equal the greater of

(i) the CRVM reserve for the underlying plan of insurance guaranteed at issue, or

(ii) the actual cash surrender value.

Also, if the statutory reserve basis is set equal to the tax reserve basis, the need for a separate tax reserve valuation is eliminated.

Definitions

GMF_t :   Guaranteed Maturity Fund at duration t. The GMF is the fund value that together with future gross premiums will cause the contract to mature based on fund guarantees.

$_tV^{CRVM}(SG)$:   CRVM reserve for the plan of insurance guaranteed at issue (secondary guarantee)

F_t :   fund value at time t

q^v :   valuation mortality rate

q^g :   guaranteed mortality rate used in fund accumulations

i^v :   valuation interest rate

i^g :   guaranteed interest rate

SC_t :   surrender charge at time t

Constraints

(1) At issue, the guaranteed projection of fund values should fall short of providing the underlying plan of insurance.

(2) $q^v \leq q^g$

(3) $i^v \geq i^g$

Case 1. In this case, $F_t \leq GMF_t$. Since $F_t \leq GMF_t$, we know that our guaranteed projection will produce smaller benefits than those provided under the secondary guarantee. Therefore, in this case, the CRVM reserve is equal to $_tV^{CRVM}(SG)$ since the guaranteed future benefits are those of the secondary guarantee and valuation net premiums are fixed.

Case 2. In this case, $F_t > GMF_t$. If $q^g = q^v$ and $i^g = i^v$, the CRVM reserve in this case would equal $_tV^{CRVM}(SG) + F_t - GMF_t$ since the present value of future benefits exceeds that used in calculating $_tV^{CRVM}(SG)$ by the excess of F_t over GMF_t, and net single premium funding is required for increases in future guaranteed benefits brought about by excess interest credits and favorable COI charges in the past.

If $q^g > q^v$ and/or $i^g < i^v$, then the CRVM reserve is less than $_tV^{CRVM}(SG) + F_t - GMF_t$, since the extra future benefits developed by the excess of F_t over GMF_t are purchased on a basis less favorable than the discount basis. Therefore, if our constraints are met,

$$_tV^{CRVM} \leq \,_tV^{CRVM}(SG) + F_t - GMF_t. \tag{D.1}$$

A set of surrender charges can be developed such that

$$F_t - SC_t \geq \,_tV^{CRVM}(SG) + F_t - GMF_t \geq \,_tV^{CRVM}. \tag{D.2}$$

Solving we find

$$SC_t \leq GMF_t - \,_tV^{CRVM}(SG). \tag{D.3}$$

GMF_t and $_tV^{CRVM}(SG)$ can be calculated at issue.

Special Notes

A similar procedure must be followed to ensure compliance with the nonforfeiture requirements of the NAIC Model Regulation for Universal Life. Special technical problems arise if the cash value accumulation test is used to qualify the product as life insurance.

Numerical Example

The calculation of Maximum Surrender Charges to guarantee that

$$MAX(_tV^{CRVM}(SG), F_t - SC_t) \geq {}_tV^{CRVM}.$$

Issue Age 35

Annual Gross Premium Per 1000:	13.83
Annual Policy Fee:	36.00
Annual Per Policy Expense Charge:	36.00
Nonforfeiture Basis:	58 CSO ALB 5.5%
Valuation Basis:	58 CSO ALB 4.5
Fund Basis:	58 CSO ALB 4.0

GMF_t: The fund value that, together with future gross premiums, is just sufficient to provide the benefits guaranteed at issue based on fund guarantees.

$$\left(A_{x+t:\overline{90-x-t|}} - 13.83 \cdot \ddot{a}_{x+t:\overline{95-x-t|}}, \text{ using 58 CSO 4.0\%} \right)$$

$CRVM(SG)$:   CRVM reserve for the secondary guarantee (E-95)

MSC_t: Maximum surrender charge at duration t

Sample Calculation

t	GMF[1]	$CRVM(SG)$[2]	MSC[3]
0	7.39	(11.36)	18.75
1	19.54	0.00	19.54
2	32.08	11.76	20.32
3	44.97	23.90	21.07
4	58.20	36.40	21.80
5	71.77	49.27	22.50
6	85.65	62.47	23.18
7	99.86	76.03	23.83
8	114.38	89.94	24.44
9	129.23	104.20	25.03
10	144.39	118.81	25.58

[1] Based on fund basis of 58 CSO 4.0%.
[2] Based on valuation basis of 58 CSO 4.5%.
[3] $GMF - CRVM(SG)$.

Since GMF and $CRVM(SG)$ are both going to 1000 at the endowment age of 95, the differential between the two (MSC) will narrow at advanced durations.

APPENDIX E

Cash Flow Projection Parameters

Projection Parameters

Projection start date: First quarter, 1990
Projection years: 25

In-force

Five years of level production (1985-1989), at 10 million per projection year.

Initial Assets

Equal to reserve at projection start date. Assets are distributed as reinvestment strategy (i.e., some percent of each type of asset as the reinvestment assets with same maturities as each type of asset; assumed to have been purchased first quarter, 1989).

Scenarios

200 random scenarios with beginning rates equal to January 1990; 90-day and 10-year rates.

Crediting Strategy

Follow competitor for four quarters, then credit 100% of net portfolio yield rate with a spread of 150 basis points, reset every quarter. Credit rate is no more than .50% higher and no less than .50% lower than the competitor rate.

Competitor Rate Definition

Maximum of

- (a) 87.5% of 2-quarter average of the 5-year scenario rate plus 1.31%, or
- (b) 82.5% of 12-quarter average of the 5-year scenario rate plus 1.25%.

Inflation Rate

100% of the 3-year scenario rate less 5% (not greater than 100% in any year).

Federal Income Tax Rates

34% of gain from operations and capital gain (negative tax allowed).

Shareholder Dividends

100% of gain from operations.

Negative Cash Flow Strategy

Borrow with 2% spread.

Excess Lapse

Exponential formula parameters:

Credited rate threshold	.50%
Multiplier	1.50
Exponent	1.50
Additional rate ratio multiplier:	.75
Reduction to additional rate multiplier:	0
Maximum total lapse rate:	30%

Base Lapse Rates

18% year 1, 12% year 2, 8% year 3, 5% thereafter (evenly distributed).

No premium adjustments formula or new business formula adjustment.

ANSWERS TO SELECTED EXERCISES

Chapter 2

2. Year 1: $\alpha_x = c_x$

Years 2-5: $P^{CRVM} = \dfrac{A_{x+1}}{\ddot{a}_{x+1}}$

Years 6-20: $P^{GRADE} = \dfrac{A_{x+5} - \left(\dfrac{A_x}{\ddot{a}_x}\right){}_{15|}\ddot{a}_{x+5} - {}_5V_x^{CRVM}}{\ddot{a}_{x+5:\overline{15|}}}$

Years 21+: $P^{NL} = \dfrac{A_x}{\ddot{a}_x}$

Chapter 3

1. Deferred premium: (a) $\dfrac{2}{12}P_x$ (b) $\dfrac{2}{12}\,\bar{a}_{\overline{1|}} \cdot \bar{P}(\bar{A}_x)$

   Net liability: (a) $\dfrac{1}{2}({}_{t-1}V_x + {}_tV_x) + \dfrac{4}{12}P_x$

     (b) $\dfrac{1}{2}\left[{}_{t-1}\bar{V}(\bar{A}_x) + {}_t\bar{V}(\bar{A}_x)\right] + \dfrac{4}{12}\bar{a}_{\overline{1|}} \cdot \bar{P}(\bar{A}_x)$

2. (c) only

4. ${}_tV^1_{x:\overline{20|}}\left(\dfrac{11}{24}\,{}_{20}P_x^{(12)}\right)$

Chapter 4

1. (a) Product A (unless both equal the cash value)
    (b) It would equal the 4% CRVM reserve for a traditional policy of the same death benefit as Product A
    (c) Product B (unless both equal the cash value)
    (d) Product A

2. (a) I   (b) III   (c) II   (d) the same   (e) III   (f) II   (g) III

Chapter 5

1. (a) $P.V.$ year 5: $10,000 \times \dfrac{1.1 \times (1.06)^2 \times (.97)}{(1.07)^3}$

    (b) $10,000 \times \dfrac{1.1 \times (1.06)^2 \times (.97)}{(1.055)^3}$

    (c) $10,000 \times \dfrac{1.1 \times (1.06) \times (1.00)}{(1.07)^2}$

    (d) $10,000 \times \dfrac{1.1 \times (1.06)^2 \times (.98)}{(1.07)^3}$

3. (a) 12,000
    (b) 10,000
    (c) 10,000
    (d) 12,000 if underlying assets are held at market, 10,000 if held at book

4. (a) $10,000 \times \dfrac{(1.09)^4 \times (.98)}{(1.07)^{3.5}}$

    (b) $10,000 \times \dfrac{(1.09)^3 \times (.98)}{(1.07)^{2.5}}$

    $$+ 10,000[(1.09)^{1.5} - (1.09)^{.5}] \dfrac{(1.09)^{2.5} \times (1.04)^2}{(1.045)^{4.5}}$$

5.   (a) $\dfrac{3401}{(1.07)^2} \times .97 - 970\ddot{a}_{\overline{2|}} = 1005$

    (b) $1048 \times \dfrac{(1.08)^2}{(1.07)^2} \times .97 = 1035$

Chapter 6

1.   (a) $15,000 \cdot {}_5V_x$

    (b) $10,000 \cdot {}_5V_x + 5000 \cdot A_{x+5}$

2.   Guaranteed minimum death benefit reserves would be required. Note that these could be much higher than for a fixed premium policy of the same general design, since the GMDB requirements for a fixed premium product include a one-year term component covering only the period of one year from the valuation date, whereas the GMDB reserves for a flexible premium policy are calculated based on the entire guarantee, without the one-year limitation.

Chapter 7

1.   (a) $(N - G)\ddot{a}_{x+t} = (14.22 - 8.60) \times 16.36 = 91.94$

    (b) $A_{x+t}^{5.5\%} - A_{x+t}^{4\%} - (G \cdot \ddot{a}_{x+t}^{5.5\%} - N \cdot \ddot{a}_{x+t}^{4\%}) = 12.41$

    (c) $A_{x+t}^{80\,CSO\,5.5\%} - A_{x+t}^{58\,CSO\,4\%} - (G \cdot \ddot{a}_{x+t}^{80\,CSO\,5.5\%} - N \cdot \ddot{a}_{x+t}^{58\,CSO\,4\%})$

$$= -123 - (-108.63)$$

Since this is less than zero, there is no deficiency reserve.

4.   It depends upon the first death status. If x and y are both alive, the Frazier reserve is the larger. If one of the two has died, then the traditional reserve is the larger.

Chapter 8

2. Because items such as loyalty of the field force and the prominence of the interest rate in marketing the policy are factors, and these items are subjective and vary from company to company.

INDEX

ABOUT THE AUTHORS

Mark A. Tullis, FSA, MAAA, is Executive Vice President and Chief Actuary of Primerica Life Insurance Company. Mark is a member of the Society of Actuary's Board of Governors. He lives in Atlanta with his wife Bettie and their two children, John and Sarah, where he enjoys bad golf, good music and brewing his own beer.

Philip K. Polkinghorn, FSA, MAAA, is a Senior Vice President, Variable Products, for First Colony Life Insurance Company. Phil is a member of the Society of Actuary's Board of Governors. He lives in Lynchburg, Virginia, with his wife Karen.